ALL YOU

F

Please return or renew this item before the latest date shown below

VF

VALLEVER D 11/18

1 0 JAN 2019

D
E

DNT

CONTENTS

PART TWO: THE WAR

PART THREE: THE AFTERMATH

For Alec and Isabel Cobbe

10 9 8 7 6 5 4 3 2 1

ISBN 978-1-911187-95-0
First published as *All you need to know: World War One*
by Connell Publishing in 2018

Picture credits:
Cover illustration © NatBasil / Shutterstock

Design: Ben Brannan
Associate Publisher: Paul Woodward
Edited by Jolyon Connell
Assistant Editor and Typesetter: Alfred Fletcher

Printed in the United Kingdom

INTRODUCTION

In its slaughter and consequences, the First World War was the most catastrophic event in 20th century European history.

For many, before 1914, a huge European war had seemed impossible. Conflicts in the Balkans flared up yet stayed contained. The Belgian historian Henri Pirenne wrote to a friend in December 1905: "Do you really believe in the possibility of a war? For me it is impossible to have the least fear in that regard." In March 1912, the British peer Lord Esher– an authority on defence matters – told an audience of Britain's senior Generals that war "becomes every day more difficult and improbable". After all, what could be gained by war? In 1909, the British writer Norman Angell claimed that with the increasing interdependence of nations war could not benefit the victor. All participating countries would be impoverished; the idea of victory was a "great illusion".

The European powers before 1914 can be caricatured: detached and complacent Britain, resentful and fearful France, militaristic or Prussian Germany, collapsing Austria-Hungary, a sick Ottoman Empire, mysterious and gigantic Russia, unreliable Italy. The rulers take on identities: "Edward the Peacemaker", the mad Emperor of Germany, the feeble Tsar of Russia, the isolated Sultan, the old and tragic Franz Joseph (ruler of the vast Hapsburg domains), the frock-coated succession of French Presidents with their concealing beards.

This sense of a puppet theatre misses the possible choices. The historian Dominic Lieven writes that in July and August 1914, "fewer than fifty individuals, all of them men, made the decisions that took their countries to war". Negotiations took place in gatherings of diplomats and politicians who not only changed their minds but were constantly changing as well. In France, there were 16 changes of foreign minister between 1906 and 1914.

In this short guide we examine controversies which have raged over the years. What caused the war? Who should be blamed for its outbreak? Should Britain have joined in and, after it did, were its soldiers really, as has been claimed, "lions led by donkeys"? What was America's role? At the end, we look at the final peace settlement. Was this as fair and sensible as possible in the circumstances or, by humiliating Germany, did the Allies pave the way to a Second World War, a truly global conflict which turned out to be even bloodier and more destructive than the First?

PART ONE:

THE CAUSES OF WAR

THE BOILING POINT.

CHAPTER ONE

THE RISE OF GERMANY

The outbreak of World War One has been called the most complex series of happenings in history and historians will always argue about what caused it.

No one, however, disputes the importance of the unification of Germany in 1871. Prussia's complete defeat of France ended with Napoleon III, a descendant of Bonaparte, going into exile and the newly united Germany (amalgamating dozens of German-speaking populations and mini-states into one country) emerging as the dominant power in continental Europe. The King of Prussia, Wilhelm I, became the Kaiser – the Emperor – of Germany, while Otto von Bismarck became its first Chancellor.

The emergence of a powerful new country in the middle of

Europe had a hugely destabilising effect. Alarm bells rang in London, where the British Prime Minister, Benjamin Disraeli, told the House of Commons that what had happened represented "a German revolution, a greater event than the French revolution of the last century". The balance of power, he said, had "been entirely destroyed, and the country which suffers most, and feels the effects of this great change most, is England".

In fact the "Iron Chancellor", Bismarck – architect of the new Germany – did not want war with England. He wished for no more wars, for his victories over Denmark, the Austro-Hungarian Empire and France had given him what he wanted. He reluctantly agreed to Prussia's annexation of Alsace and Lorraine in France, suspecting, rightly, that it would cause simmering resentment. He saw the vulnerability of a new Germany surrounded by hostile nations and, to safeguard her eastern border, arranged a treaty with Russia in 1887, each power promising to remain netural towards the other. He showed great diplomatic skill in keeping France isolated, while reassuring Britain that the new German empire would not be a threat to her security or empire.

But Bismarck's system depended on one man: Bismarck. He had an acquiescent master in Kaiser Wilhelm I and an iron control of parliament. In the new German constitution, foreign policy, defence and the choice of ministers stayed in the hands of the crown.

The situation changed with the accession of Kaiser Wilhelm II to the throne in 1888. A grandson of Queen Victoria, the new Kaiser was autocratic and emotionally unstable. Lord Salisbury, by now British prime minister, wondered if he was "all there". Wilhelm II, unlike his predecessor, wanted to rule as well as reign. He dismissed Bismarck in 1890, turned his ministers into little more than messengers, or functionaries, and rapidly proved, "as the loosest of cannons, that he was not up to the job".

While Bismarck had been content merely to preserve the new German empire, the new Kaiser was not so easily satisfied. He embodied, in the view of the eminent historian, Professor Sir Michael Howard, three qualities that can be said to have characterised the then ruling elite: "archaic militarism, vaulting ambition, and neurotic insecurity".

Germany, like Prussia before her, was a militaristic culture. "It became good form even for the higher state officials to wear military uniform at every conceivably fitting occasion," notes Gerhard Ritter. The philosopher Heinrich von Treitschke, a bitter enemy of the British Empire, declared that Prussia's greatness had come about through war. In Treitschke's lectures in Berlin, attended by the future Field Marshal Hindenburg and the future Admiral Tirpitz, Darwin's theory of "natural selection" was applied to nations. "Weak and cowardly peoples go to the wall," Treitschke said, "and rightly so. In this everlasting contest of different states lies the beauty of History and to wish to abolish this conflict is sheer nonsense." War was vital "as a terrible medicine for mankind"; peace a dream of "weary, dispirited and worn-out ears".

On its own, the Kaiser's militarism might have been merely absurd, with the constant parades and endless celebrations of victories, but it was made dangerous by his ambition. Certainly many of his contemporaries, including several European statesmen, thought him mildly unhinged. Christopher Clark writes:

He was an extreme exemplar of that Edwardian social category, the club bore who is forever explaining some pet project to the man in the next chair. Small wonder that being button-holed by the Kaiser over lunch or dinner, when escape was impossible, struck fear into the hearts of so many European royals.

Winston Churchill, a guest at German military manoeuvres before the war, admired Wilhelm's "undeniable cleverness" but worried about his inadequate temperament. All Europe's monarchs were "wild cards in the doom game played out in 1914", says Max Hastings, "but Wilhelm was the wildest of all".

So Bismarck's legacy to his country ended up as a dysfunctional political system in which the will of the German people (expressed through the liberal-minded Reichstag, their parliament), was trumped by the powers of the Emperor, his appointed ministers and the army's chief of staff. Jonathan Steinberg writes:

Bismarck… left a system which only he – a very abnormal person – could govern and then only if he had as superior a normal Kaiser. [Thereafter] neither condition obtained, and the system slithered into the sycophancy, intrigue and bluster that made the Kaiser's Germany a danger to its neighbours.

Wilhelm II, the last German Emperor (Kaiser)

Germany's right-wing leadership now began to claim for Germany the status of a World Power, or *Weltmacht*. This led to a World Policy, or *Weltpolitik*, aimed at expanding Berlin's influence. The Reinsurance Treaty between Germany and Russia, arranged by Bismarck, was allowed to lapse – in hindsight, a critical error. Russia edged closer to France; by 1894 the two countries were formally in alliance. "That young man [the Kaiser] wants war with Russia," Bismarck told an aide before his dismissal, "and would like to draw his sword straight away if he could."

Viewed from Moscow or Paris, the alliance between the French and the Russians was a sensible precaution, given Germany's alliance with Austria-Hungary. But viewed from Berlin, as tensions grew in the early years of the 20th century, and Britain emerged as a possible third partner, the amity between France and Rus-

GERMAN MILITARISM

Fritz Stern calls pre-1914 Germany "a thoroughly militaristic country". Bethmann-Hollweg, in his first appearance at the Reichstag as Chancellor in 1909, wore a major's uniform. "Only the person who could wear the uniform with the silver epaulettes counted as a real man," says Gerhard Ritter. The Kaiser much preferred the company of soldiers to diplomats and politicians.

A cult of honour and physical courage existed in Germany long before 1914. It is widely accepted to have been the most militarised country in Europe, even if by one measure – the proportion of the population under arms – France was in the lead, with 2.29 per cent in the army and navy compared to Germany's 1.33 per cent. In Germany, the spirit of the Enlightenment – the emphasis on rationalism and the intellect – was much weaker, even despised. Philosophers such as Fichte and Nietzsche, and Wagner, the composer, turned from rationalism to feeling, mystery and an admiration for power.

Duelling was still acceptable in both Germany and France. In German universities, the deep scars etched on to cheeks in fencing matches were badges of honour. Clemenceau, wartime Prime Minister of France, fought several duels.

sia came to seem much more threatening. So the power blocks of 1914 formed, amidst growing German anxiety about encirclement: France to the west, Russia to the east, Britain at sea.

Meanwhile, the new country was taking off. Between 1871 and 1914 Germany's growth was staggering. Its population rose from 40 million to 65 million and its achievements were extraordinary. "In 1914, Berlin was the Athens of the world," says Norman Stone, "a place where you went to learn anything important – physics, philosophy, music, engineering…"

Three members of the British cabinet which went to war in 1914 had studied at German universities. One of these, the war minister, Lord Haldane, described Germany in 1912 as "already one of the greatest nations in the world in virtue of character and intellectual endowment". German chemists and engineers were noted for their ingenuity, and Germany and its allies came close to victory in the Italian mountains because Ferdinand Porsche invented the four-wheel drive to deal with them (before going on to invent Volkswagen and much else). Industry boomed. "In 1914 the great smokestacks of the Ruhr predominated, as once those of… Manchester had done."

CHAPTER TWO

CHALLENGING BRITAIN AT SEA

The confidence of the Germans grew – and success went to their heads. Bismarck had always been cautious, worrying about Germany's potential isolation. The Kaiser, however, had no such doubts. His "model" was rich Britain with her huge empire and powerful navy. I adore England," the Kaiser told Theodore Roosevelt. He corresponded in fluent English and read P.G. Wodehouse aloud to his inner circle, laughing uproariously. Why shouldn't Germany match Britain's empire and her navy? Although overjoyed when, shortly after his accession, his grandmother Queen Victoria made him an honorary British admiral, the Kaiser was jealous of British imperial self-confidence. He urged his military advisers to read Alfred Mahan's book, The Influence of Sea Power upon History, and spent hours drawing sketches of ships he thought should be built.

Having allowed her alliance with Russia to slip, and with France and Russia now allies, the last thing that Germany needed was a problem with Britain. Norman Stone believes "the greatest mistake of the twentieth century was made when Germany built a navy designed to attack her". The decision to create a fleet capable of challenging the Royal Navy and to reject the continental balance of power, the cornerstone of British foreign policy, put Berlin on an increasingly dangerous path. It was very much the Kaiser's personal commitment, and strongly opposed by the army.

The naval arms race began in 1898, when Germany passed the first of its Naval Laws.* Admiral von Tirpitz, the commander of the High Seas Fleet, assured the Kaiser that his plans would be so successful that they would "concede to Your Majesty such a measure of naval mastery [as to] enable Your Majesty to carry out a great overseas policy". On the contrary, it was a disastrous policy, wrecking relations with London. "Although there were other milestones along the path of the growth of enmity and suspicion between Britain and Germany, such as the Kaiser's noisy support for the Boers [during the Boer War in South Africa], the avowed German challenge to British naval security was the most important single factor."

For centuries, Britain had sought to prevent any one power dom-

---

* Five separate Naval Laws were passed between 1898 and 1912, committing Germany to building what the Kaiser wanted: "as fine a navy as the English".

inating continental Europe: with a powerful navy but a small army (Bismarck once observed with scorn that if her all-volunteer force landed on the continent he would send a policeman to arrest it), Britain was determined that the Low Countries – the Netherlands and Belgium – should not fall into the hands of a hostile power.

Britain's traditional rivals were France and Russia. Hitherto, Britain's relations with Germany had largely been friendly: the 18th century rise of Prussia had been welcomed as a counterbalance to France; Frederick the Great's campaigns were partly financed by the British; Britain was full of pubs called The King of Prussia, and there was even a sense of racial similarity. Cecil Rhodes included Germans in his scholarships scheme for Oxford because of their Anglo-Saxon blood. Admiral von Tirpitz employed an English governess for his daughters, sending them to finish their education at Cheltenham Ladies College.

The naval race changed everything, not least British public opinion about Germany. Crucially, it also caused Britain to mend her fences with her traditional rivals. In 1904 she settled her differences with France in Africa, beginning a relationship which became known as the Entente Cordiale; three years later she had a rapprochement with Russia, which had been weakened and brought to the verge of revolution by an unsuccessful war with Japan (1904-5) and was now happy to reach an agreement with Britain over the disputed borderlands of Persia and Afghanistan.

Thus was born the Triple Entente between France, Britain and Russia. Britain's accommodation with Russia fell short of a formal alliance, as did her commitment to France, but to the Germans it looked very much as if a power block had been formed and that the British were "weaving a web to encircle and imprison them".

By 1914, moreover, Britain had moved ahead in the naval race. Germany was in a bind: a third of her defence budget had been allocated to finance new ships, while the army, with less money available, was in no position to fight the two-front war which the Franco-Russian alliance might render necessary. Germany's army in 1914 was barely larger than France's, although France's population was some 25 million less than Germany's. German battleships, meanwhile, were well built but there were too few of them. They were destined to spend almost the entire First World War in harbour, until, at the end, the crews mutinied, sealing Germany's defeat and bringing an end to the Kaiser's empire.

In the pre-war years, relations between Germany and Britain steadily worsened. When, in 1911, the Germans challenged French influence in Morocco by staging a show of naval strength at Agadir, Britain was openly supportive of France. Thereafter, the feeling began to grow in both Germany and Britain that war was highly likely, if not inevitable.

The year of the Agadir crisis also saw the publication of *Germany and the Next War*, by a retired German general, Frederick von Bernhardi. This had run to six editions by 1913, spreading alarm through Europe. War, Bernhardi wrote, had made Prussia. Now it could make Germany a "mighty" European state and a world power. Frederick the Great had, rightly, sought war; the British concept of the balance of power was nonsense, typical of a weak country. Out-of-date treaties need not be observed. There were two options for Germany: world power or defeat.

THE ROLE OF IMPERIALISM

In 1895 the young sociologist Max Weber, who had resigned from Germany's Pan-German League because he thought it not nationalist enough, gave a lecture which Norman Stone describes as "one of the stupidest" ever given by "a clever man". (Stone, p12) England, Weber said, has no social problems because she is rich; she is rich because of her empire; she has her empire because she has a great navy; a great navy is therefore a good idea and England would accept Germany having an imperial role if she, too, had a great navy.

Every step in his argument was wrong, including the idea that empires make you rich.

At the end of European imperialism, in the 1970s, the poorest country in the continent was Portugal, which ran a huge African empire, and the richest were Sweden, which abandoned its only colony – in the Caribbean – long before, and Switzerland, which never had an empire at all. (Stone, p12)

At the outbreak of World War One, Britain was the world's greatest imperial power. Germany had only some odds and ends in Africa and the Pacific, a pathetic contrast with Britain and France: "even little bourgeois Belgium had the immense Congo". (Macmillan, *The war That Ended Peace*, p82) The great Bismarck, however, had never been interested in colonies, seeing them as an expensive distraction. "My map of Africa lies here in Europe," he told an explorer in 1888. "Here lies Russia," he said, pointing at a map, "and here lies France, and we are right in the middle; this is my map of Africa."

On the face of it, says Hew Strachan, Germany had a much greater interest in taking the war beyond Europe than Britain did; Britain's overseas possessions were more vulnerable to attack than Britain itself. Germany's "enthusiasm for widening the conflict was not principally a form of covert imperialism. It was a way of fighting the war." (Strachan, p79)

By 1918, it is true, the victors had gained control of additional territory, not least large parts of the dismembered Ottoman Empire. Japan, declaring war on Germany in August, 1914, seized her islands in the Central Pacific – the Marshalls, the Marianas and the Carolines – and her base, Tsingtao, on the Chinese mainland. Australia and New Zealand grabbed other German islands in the South Pacific. There was fierce fighting in Africa, too, with British and French successes in Togoland and the Cameroons.

But this was not so much driven by imperialism per se as "the by-product of a war that had begun for different reasons". (Sheffield, p12) Territory was picked up from the defeated nations "almost out of force of habit, as for example the British had done in the Seven Years War a century and a half earlier. That was what empires did."

CHAPTER THREE

'DESPERATE BUT NOT SERIOUS'

While Germany was relatively united, its rickety ally, Austria-Hungary, was not. Explosive nationalism haunted Europe in the years before the war, nowhere more so than in the vast Hapsburg Empire. This ramshackle entity, made up of some 50 million people of 11 different nationalities, seethed with disputed territories and discontented minorities: Romanians in Hungary, Czechs in Hapsburg Bohemia and Moravia, Hungarians objecting to diktats from Vienna, northern Italians unhappy in Austria, Poles still angry about the 18th-century partitioning of their country. Nationalism posed a threat not just to the Hapsburg

Empire's cohesion but to its very existence.

Austria, after its 1866 defeat by the Prussians, became Austria-Hungary the following year. The creation of the so-called "Dual Monarchy" was an attempt to deal with nationalist feeling in Hungary. It gave Hungarians their own government, though foreign and financial policy continued to be shared with Austria under the control of the Hapsburg crown. But while this new constitution may have been useful in addressing the issue of Hungarian identity, it failed to address the wider problem of differences between other ethnic groups in the empire – a problem exacerbated by a huge, multi- ethnic and vastly expensive bureaucracy. New railway stations went unnamed because of disagreements about which language to use. In the Dual Monarchy's parliaments political parties divided on linguistic and ethnic lines.

> Deputies blew trumpets, rang cowbells, banged gongs, beat on drums and hurled inkpots and books around to silence their opponents. [On one occasion] a German deputy spoke for 12 straight hours during the struggle to stop Czech being given equal status with German in Bohemia and Moravia. "In our country," a conservative aristocrat wrote to a friend, "an optimist must commit suicide."

But somehow the empire – the "corpse on the Danube", as Austria-Hungary was sometimes called – survived, its situation, in the words of a Viennese joke, "desperate but not serious".

Restless and unstable, it constantly sought to take advantage of the decline of the once powerful Ottoman Empire (now Turkey) and increase its influence in the Balkans. Bismarck, conscious of

Balkan Region, 1870s
— Nations
- - - Disputed boundaries
· · · · Aquatic borders

the danger of a Balkan war, brokered an agreement at the Congress of Berlin in 1878 which divided the region into spheres of influence between Russia and the Dual Monarchy. Under the terms of Bismarck's treaty, the Austro-Hungarians were to be allowed to occupy the Ottoman provinces of Bosnia-Herzegovina. This caused huge resentment from Balkan nationalists, especially in the independent state of Serbia, which believed it should be the ruler of all Serbs, many of whom lived in Bosnia-Herzegovina.

With Russia, a defender of the Serbs, hovering in the background the situation was fraught with danger and Bismarck's attempt to defuse it was never likely to be successful for long. Tensions rose further in 1908 when Vienna, in an attempt to curb Serbian power, formally annexed Bosnia-Herzegovina.

Germany and Austria-Hungary were the main components of

what became known as the Triple Alliance. Berlin's dependence on this, though far from ideal, was forced upon it by its own diplomatic incompetence in alienating both France and Russia. The third member of the Alliance, Italy, was highly unreliable and the signs were clear that Austria-Hungary would soon disintegrate. "In an age of nationalism, this vast, multi-national empire was an anachronism (there were fifteen versions of the imperial anthem, the Gott Erhalte, including a Yiddish one)."

The Kaiser believed he had no option but to stand by the Hapsburgs; if the Austro-Hungarian empire fell, Russia and her client states in the Balkans would be the beneficiaries. In December 1912 Wilhelm told the Swiss ambassador in Berlin: "we will not leave Austria in the lurch: if diplomacy fails we shall have to fight this racial war". And though the empire was tottering long before war broke out, it had shown it could compromise and survive. For many, the ancient Emperor Franz Joseph was still a symbol of protection, especially to the minorities under his rule.

Franz Joseph had been on the throne since 1848 – murmuring, as the coronation ceremony began: "Farewell my youth!" – and had created the Dual Monarchy in 1867. Pre-1914 Vienna may have been home to modernist geniuses such as Mahler and Freud, but at its centre, toiling over memoranda, sleeping in a narrow bed in one of his huge palaces, was this old, unimaginative, slightly dim figure.

His wife, the beautiful and vain Empress Elizabeth, had become increasingly unresponsive before her assassination in 1898. For years Franz Joseph had led a life of pleasant domesticity with an actress called Katharina Schratt. "At Ischl, his summer residence, [he] rambled alone to her house, Villa Felicitas, where he would sometimes arrive at 7 a.m. after sending a note: 'Please leave the small door unlocked.'" But this romance was over by 1914.

Once a soldier, Franz Joseph saw the army as the unifying force of the empire. The army, however, was poorly led. "Its officer corps was dominated by noblemen, most of whom combined conceit with incompetence."

Vienna, the capital of the Empire, was the most cosmopolitan and cultured city in Europe. In one of those curious accidents of history Stalin, Trotsky, Tito and Hitler all spent some months there in 1913. The middle classes thrived while the aristocratic Viennese lived an almost feudal lifestyle – housemaids were entitled to only seven hours off a fortnight. Beneath the glittering surface there was poverty and unemployment, as there was throughout the empire, and the fashionable Viennese seemed as oblivious as their Emperor of the forces of history threatening their world.

The Hapsburg Monarchy was "a system of institutionalised escapism", in Norman Stone's apt phrase. Its generals "regarded war with reckless insouciance, as a mere tool for the advancement of national interests rather than as a passport to Hades".

CHAPTER FOUR

WAS SERBIA A ROGUE STATE?

Serbia had been outraged by Vienna's annexation of Bosnia-Herzegovina in 1908, seeing it both as an expansion of Austrian power and a threat to Slavic independence in the Balkans. But Serbia's victories in the Balkan Wars of 1912-13 – over the Ottoman Empire, then Bulgaria – caused the balance of power to swing again, with Serbia gaining a huge area of land, doubling her population and territory and becoming one of the largest states in southern Europe, as well as the strongest military power in the Balkans.

By now relations between Serbia and Austria were bad. Austria-Hungary feared encirclement by Russia and a league of hostile Balkan Slav states. France supported Serbia, which was also emboldened by pledges from Russia. So the German promise to Austria-Hungary, and the French and Russian promise to Serbia, ensured a potential widening of any dispute in the Balkans. This was the situation when, on June 28th 1914, the heir to the Hapsburg throne, Archduke Franz Ferdinand, was assassinated in the Serbian capital of Sarajevo.

There was an element of farce about the killing. Seven Serbian terrorists, who had gathered in the city during the preceding days, spread themselves out along the Archduke's likely route. With bombs no bigger than cakes of soap strapped to their waists and loaded revolvers in their pockets, they awaited the cars carrying the royal party. The first attempt to kill the heir to the Hapsburg throne went badly wrong when a bomb flung by an assassin fell short of its target, injuring several officers in the car behind and, slightly, the Archduke's wife, Sophie, whose cheek was cut by a splinter. Franz Ferdinand was unharmed. Foolishly, but with remarkable sang-froid, he insisted the visit continue as planned. "Come on," he said. "That fellow is clearly insane; let us proceed with our programme."

After a visit to the town hall the Archduke decided to go to the hospital to see an officer who had been wounded by the bomb. But no one told his driver of the change of plan. The car was driven into the wrong street and so had to reverse, a slow process in those days. This gave another of the young terrorists, Gavrilo Princip, waiting in front of a shop, his chance; seeing the car stall, Princip caught up with it, drew his revolver and fired twice at point blank range. The Archduke and Sophie (who had been celebrating their wedding anniversary) were both killed.

Serbia had long been seen as a menace in the chancelleries of Western Europe. Her self-assertiveness, summed up in the popular catchphrase "Where a Serb dwells, there is Serbia" destabilised the Balkans. Many European statesmen "were irritated by its little Serbia proud-victim culture". All the major continental powers knew that the Serbs could only achieve their goal of assimilating their two million brethren living under Hapsburg rule by destroying the Austro-Hungarian Empire.

Those who argue that Serbia was essentially a rogue state, such as the historian Christopher Clark, point to her history in the years before 1914. Clark begins his book *The Sleepwalkers* with a vivid account of the events of June 11, 1903, when the country's ruling Obrenovic dynasty was overthrown in a particularly bloody coup.

A group of armed conspirators broke into the royal palace where, having failed to find King Alexandar and Queen Draga in their bedchamber, they strode from room to room "firing at cabinets, tapestries, sofas and other potential hiding places". While they continued the search, other victims, including the Queen's two sisters and the prime minister, were found and killed elsewhere in Belgrade. Eventually, back in the palace, the royal couple, who had been hiding in a tiny annexe off the bedchamber, were found and "cut down in a hail of shots at point-blank range". The corpses were stabbed with swords and partly disembowelled. The body of the Queen, "virtually naked and slimy with gore", was tossed from the bedroom window into the gardens.

The end of the Obrevonic dynasty, and the succession to the throne of Peter Karadjordjevic, led to a much more aggressive regime in Belgrade, dedicated to the liberation of Serbs under foreign rule, especially those in Bosnia. The new king had much less power than the old. The conspirators, centred on the army, who had come together to murder the royal family, remained "an important force in Serbian politics and public life". The king was really the "prisoner" of those who had brought him to power.

When Vienna formally annexed Bosnia-Herzegovina in 1908, the Serbian government reacted by creating an open "liberation movement" or Bosnian Serbs. At the heart of this was a covert terrorist wing – "The Black Hand" – trained and supported by elements of the Serbian army. Among them was a young lieutenant, Dragutin Dimitrijevic, who became known as "Apis" because his heavy build "reminded admirers of the broad-shouldered bull god of ancient Egypt". An obsessively secretive and dedicated nationalist, Apis had played a key role in the conspiracy to kill the king and queen in 1903. He was also the driving force behind the plot to kill the Archduke Franz Ferdinand in 1914, an operation organised by the Black Hand.

But was Serbia really a rogue, or at least a failing, state? Arguably, as Gary Sheffield says, the fact that the Serbian Prime Minister, Nicholas Pasic, was unable to stop "the renegade Apis" from sending death squads on to Hapsburg territory suggests that it was. But several points can be made in mitigation. First, there was no evidence at the time that this was state-sponsored terrorism; the connection between Apis and the assassins didn't become clear until later. Moreover, Pasic, who got wind of the plot, tried to warn the Austrians – although his warning was too vague to be useful.

Nor did Austria-Hungary's reaction to the killings seem to support the view that Serbia was out of control. Instead of acting immediately, it did nothing for three weeks. Then the government in Vienna sent a draconian ultimatum – "the most formidable document I have ever seen addressed from one state to another," in the view of Sir Edward Grey, the British Foreign Secretary – most of which Serbia promptly accepted.

The charges made in the ultimatum about the participation of the Black Hand were not denied. But Clauses 5 and 6, which decreed that the Austrians should be allowed to investigate and arbitrate on Serbian soil, amounted to nothing less than a demand that Serbia surrender her sovereignty, something no nation could readily concede. Max Hastings finds that while the "irresponsibility of Serbian behaviour is almost indisputable" it still "seems extravagant, on the evidence, to brand the country a rogue state, deserving of destruction".

The Austrians, however, were determined to use the killings in Sarajevo as the pretext to crush the Serbian enemy once and for all. The hawks in Vienna, confident of German support, quickly declared their intentions. Prominent among them was the Austrian Chief of Staff, Conrad von Hötzendorf, who said: "We have to go for all or nothing. In 1912-13 it would have been a game with some chances of success, now it is a sheer gamble." War must come "for so ancient a monarchy and so glorious an army cannot be allowed to perish ignominiously".

Conrad von Hötzendorf was intense and vain; he never wore his glasses if he could help it. Often shy in company, he liked walking alone in the mountains, "where he produced melancholy pencil sketches of steep slopes shrouded in dark conifers". His devotion to duty had been instilled in him by his mother who always denied him supper until he had finished his homework.

Christopher Clark calls him "one of the most intriguing figures to hold high military office in early twentieth-century Europe". Appointed chief of the General Staff in 1906, he was an aggressive advocate of war against Austria-Hungary's enemies.

After the death of his wife in 1905, Conrad began a potentially scandalous relationship with Gina von Reininghaus, who was married to a Viennese industrialist. The pair met at a Vienna dinner party in 1907; a week or so later Conrad arrived at the Reininghaus villa and announced to his hostess: "I am terribly in love with you and have only one thought in my head: that you

THE RISE OF NATIONALISM

The influence of Charles Darwin's *Origin of Species* (1859) was strong in Europe in 1914. Social Darwinism – which applied Darwin's theory of the survival of the fittest to society – reinforced older philosophies of competitive individualism, such as those of the philosopher Thomas Hobbes, who saw international relations as "nothing more than an endless jockeying for advantage among nations".

Along with competitive individualism came racism – a contempt for the weak. Ludwig Woltmann, a social anthropologist, developed a theory that the Germans were Teutons while the French were Celts, an inferior race. Woltmann even explained France's former triumphs as having been achieved by what was left of
the French race's Teutonic roots. In Germany, Britain and France the new mass media and hundreds of popular novels glorified past military history. Great victories were celebrated in festivals, monuments and place names (like London's Waterloo Station and Trafalgar Square).

"We learnt," said a distinguished British soldier, "to believe that the English were the salt of the earth and England the first and greatest country in the world. Our confidence in her powers and our utter disbelief in the possibility of any earthly Power vanquishing her, became a fixed idea which nothing could eradicate and no gloom dispel." (Macmillan, *The War That Ended Peace*, p250)

In France, a manual for schoolchildren extolled the beauty of France and the ideals of the French revolution; the purpose of history, children were taught, was to instill patriotism. War was seen as glamorous. Long immunity from its realities had "blunted our imaginations", as one British liberal put it. The conservative Catholic writer Hilaire Belloc wrote: "How I long for the Great War! It will sweep Europe like a broom, it will make kings jump like coffee beans on the roaster." (Macmillan, p265)

In Germany, the ardent nationalist

should become my wife." She turned him down. But he became obsessed, threatening to resign his post if she wouldn't marry him. Eventually they reached a compromise (she might marry him, but not yet) and began an affair, during which he wrote hundreds of love letters to her, sometimes several a day, telling her she was his sole joy.

Human passions play an important, if often unrecognised, part in international affairs. It would be difficult, says Christopher Clark,

General Friedrich von Bernhardi argued that his country needed more space (an idea the Nazis developed in the notion of Lebensraum, "living space"). Imperialism, in Bernhardi's view, was vital to increase power. Britain was envied as it celebrated Empire Day, with children drawing union jacks and hanging up flags of the dominions in their classrooms. The German Chancellor, Bethmann-Hollwegg, told the French ambassador to Berlin in January 1914 that France had long pursued a "grandiose policy" while Germany had been inactive: "today it needs its place in the sun". (Macmillan, p252) French intellectuals had long speculated about the German, or Prussian, character. Had the "dreary Prussian landscape and the grey weather", it was wondered, made Prussians "a dour, grasping people"?

A convincing account of the war's more profound (or "subterranean") causes came in 1929, when the French historian Elie Halevy gave the Rhodes lectures at Oxford. Halevy, too old for active service, had been in a French ambulance unit and seen terrible suffering. Now he looked for "the collective forces, the collective feelings and movements of public opinion, which, in the early years of the twentieth century, made for strife".

To Halevy, nationalism was the great danger. He argued that the assassination in July 1914 of Jean Jaures, the French socialist leader and persuasive internationalist, had made it harder to cool nationalist feeling across Europe.

to overstate the importance of this relationship; it was at the centre of Conrad's life throughout the years from 1907 to the outbreak of war, eclipsing all other concerns… He even came to see the war as a means of gaining possession of Gina. Only as a victorious war hero, Conrad believed, would he be able to sweep aside the social obstacles and the scandal attaching to a marriage with a prominent divorcee.

Conrad called repeatedly for war against Serbia, telling his mistress in 1909: "It is a crime that nothing is being done. War against Serbia could have saved the monarchy." He was, writes Norman Stone, "one of the men primarily responsible for the outbreak of the First World War". So vehemently did he make his case that he was even dismissed from his post by the Emperor in December 1911 – though after a year he was reinstated, only to return immediately to the offensive, counselling a Serbian war no less than 25 times during 1913.

The assassinations in Sarajevo finally gave him the pretext that he needed. The irony was that the Archduke had been Austria-Hungary's foremost advocate of peace. Tall and handsome – if his moustache was not quite a match for the Kaiser's, "it nevertheless twirled smartly into sharp points" – Franz Ferdinand hated Jews, Freemasons, Hungarians and Serbs ("pigs"). When shooting he liked to have "great quantities" of game driven towards him as he shot "until his guns turned red hot". It is said that he once suddenly demanded a herd of deer be rounded up and "shot all 200 of them as well as one of the beaters by mistake".

His relationship with the Emperor was never warm. He had only become heir to the throne after the Emperor's son, Crown

Prince Rudolf, committed suicide in 1889, and the Emperor always treated him with condescension. The Emperor also thoroughly disapproved of his marriage to the Czech noblewoman Sophie Chotek, feeling she was not grand enough for a Hapsburg; Sophie was "not permitted to join her husband in the royal box at the opera, sit near him at gala dinners, or accompany him in the splendid royal carriage with its golden wheels".

But he was intellectually curious, very influential in Vienna and well-informed. "It is one of the smaller tragedies of the summer of 1914," writes Margaret Macmillan, "that in assassinating Franz Ferdinand the Serb nationalists removed the one man in Austria-Hungary who might have prevented it going to war."

Austria-Hungary declared war on July 28. Its leaders didn't give a "fig" for the persons of the slain Archduke and his "embarrassing wife", but the murders "represented the best justification they would ever have for settling accounts with a mortally troublesome neighbour". War was decided on because, for the Emperor and his ministers, it "was the only way out of their difficulties, not merely with Serbia, but with their own restless peoples". "We decided on war quite early," the Austrian finance minister said later. If any country behaved like "a rogue state" in the summer of 1914, argues Gary Sheffield, that country was Austria-Hungary. "It is clear that a large measure of the responsibility for bringing about the First World War belongs to Austria-Hungary."

CHAPTER FIVE

BLAMING GERMANY

Afterwards, the victors, naturally, blamed Germany, citing her aggression, her militarism, her wish to dominate Europe, her mad emperor – hence the name frequently given to the First World War: "the Kaiser's war". Germany's invasion of Belgium lost her the high ground. The violation of Belgian neutrality was a crime under international law, followed later by the unrestricted U-Boat campaign. The victors did not mention the British naval blockade – arguably also illegal under international law – which had brought the Central Powers to the point of starvation.

Many Germans thought that the rest of Europe had failed, from envy or fear, to accommodate their new power. They were encircled by enemies and had no alternative but to go to war. Their one

THE MOROCCAN CRISES

The two Moroccan crises of 1905 and 1911 strengthened the Entente Cordiale between France and Britain and deepened the distrust between the Entente and Germany.

In the spring of 1905, the Kaiser anchored off Tangier in his yacht. His advisers, who resented French influence over Morocco, urged him to go ashore. So Wilhelm – on a white Arabian which he found difficult to mount because it shied at the sight of his helmet – rode through the narrow streets to see the Sultan.

During his visit he insisted that Morocco was an independent country, belligerently adding that France would be expected to recognise Germany's interests there. Wilhelm's advisers hoped that this assertion of German ambitions might lead to the collapse of the Franco-British alliance and even cause Britain to tilt towards Germany. But it had the opposite effect. The Entente hardened. Britain began to worry more about Germany.

The crisis was defused by the Algeciras conference of 1906. This confirmed Morocco's independence though did little to change the status quo. Five years later, trouble blew up again. In April 1911, the French sent troops into Morocco, ostensibly to deal with riots in Fez. The move angered Berlin and this time, as Margaret Macmillan says, the Germans had a good case. (Macmillan, p414) The French had already flouted the spirit of the Algeciras treaty by trying to establish economic and political dominance over Morocco; now

they were failing to consult the treaty's other signatories, including Germany, before sending in troops. But once again the German reaction was clumsy: they sent a small gunboat, the Panther, to anchor off the port of Agadir.

This alarmed the British government, which made clear its determination to support France. The crisis was eventually defused with another treaty – the Treaty of Fez – under the terms of which France was given the right to establish a protectorate over Morocco, though with the commitment to respect German economic interests. Germany was given 100,000 square miles of central Africa.

But the clash cast a long shadow. Once again a resentful Germany felt that it had been defeated. As Sir Edward Grey later said: "The consequences of such a foreign crisis do not end with it. They seem to end but they go underground and reappear later on."

El-Hadj el-Mokri, Moroccan Ambassador to Spain, signs the treaty at the Algeciras Conference 7 April, 1906.

reliable ally was the tottering Austro-Hungarian Empire. They felt they must support the aggressive Austrian reaction to Serbia after the assassinations at Sarajevo.

The three men making the crucial decisions in Berlin were the Kaiser, Bethmann-Hollweg, the Chancellor, and Helmuth van Moltke, the chief of staff, who controlled the most powerful military machine in Europe. None of them made any attempt to avert the crisis or prevent it getting out of hand. Instead Berlin actively encouraged the Austrians to attack Serbia. A diplomat dispatched from Vienna to Berlin on July 4 was promised Germany's unconditional support for whatever Austria chose to do: this was the so-called "blank cheque" which later became central to the case of those who blamed Germany for the war.

And the Germans were more than supportive; they sought to force the pace, urging the Austrians to act. Moltke was prone to melancholy, played the cello and was fascinated by the afterlife and the occult. He was by no means a typical general. But he had long believed that Germany's salvation lay in war. As early as 1912 he and the Kaiser had assured Franz Ferdinand that he could always depend on German support.

Bethmann-Hollweg 's reputation is one of vacillation, but he shared Moltke's paranoia about the Russian threat, and the feeling that it would have to be dealt with sooner rather than later. A bureaucrat rather than a politician, he worried that he might be thought weak in comparison with Bismarck and contemplated resigning before the war, feeling threatened by militant figures such as Moltke and Admiral Tirpitz. He stayed, believing that he could stop them from forcing the pace. He showed his pessimism, however, by stopping the planting of slow-growing lime trees on

Conrad von Hötzendorf, Chief of the General Staff of the military from 1906-1917

his Brandenburg estate because invaders would benefit from them: a prophecy fulfilled when the Red Army arrived in 1945. Fritz Stern asks:

> Is it not likely that Bethmann's resolution in July 1914 was strengthened by a feeling that his policy of so-called conciliatoriness had yielded nothing, strengthened by the weariness of the civilian who had for so long been attacked by his tougher colleagues?

The strain of fatalism in the German character was also prominent in Moltke. In late July 1914, he was arguing that delay could be fatal. Russia and France were moving towards mobilisation; each lost day made the German position more perilous. Yet war, Moltke believed, must "annihilate for decades the civilisation of almost all Europe". General Eric von Falkenhayn, who succeeded him as Chief of Staff, thought that "[even] if everything goes smash, it will have been worth it". Max Weber, a philosopher and sociologist, showed a similar mixture of doubt and enthusiasm. "Regardless of eventual success," he told a friend in August 1914, "this war is great and wonderful." But by October Weber was writing about "the hundreds of thousands who are bleeding because of the appalling incompetence of our diplomacy".

After the Armistice in 1918, each side nursed its version of what caused the war, and when, more than 40 years later, revisionism came from one of their own historians, Germans reacted with horror. Following long archival research, Fritz Fischer published his *Griff nach der Weltmacht* ("Bid for World Power") in October 1961. Fischer's book claimed that there had been a German militaristic conspiracy, that Germany was to blame, that her quest for power and her aggression had led to war.

Outrage followed, in German universities, in the press and in public life. Attacked by members of his own profession, Fischer had the grant for a lecture tour of the United States withdrawn by the German Foreign Office. He received threatening telephone calls and was publicly insulted. One of his opponents, the conservative historian Gerhard Ritter, broke down while giving a lecture in Freiburg that tried to refute his arguments. To Ritter, who had resisted the Nazis (Fischer had been a member of the party between 1939 and 1942), the new book's claims were an affront to German identity, still reeling from the horrific revelations of wartime atrocities and the Holocaust. Ritter admitted that the military had had a pernicious influence before 1914 but held that the then Chancellor, Bethmann-Hollweg, had been a man of peace. For German historians schooled in the tradition that the Nazi regime was an aberration, Fischer admitted, "my book was nothing short of treason".

In the decades since, his views have been vigorously and, in some respects, convincingly challenged. For example, he argued that the rise of the Social Democrats in the Reichstag elections of 1912 dismayed the military hawks in Germany, making the Imperial government decide that war was the best way to unite the country behind the government. "The war provided an opportunity to assert and strengthen the old social and political order," as Fischer put it. This view – that Germany's domestic troubles were an important motivating factor – has not won much support, nor has his emphasis on the decision of the so-called 'War Council' on December 8, 1912, to start a war, though not for another 18 months. His picture of Bethmann-Hollweg as a precursor to Hitler has been dismissed as far-fetched.

And was there really as much cool premeditation in Berlin as historians of the Fischer school suggest? Wasn't German policy-making more erratic? War loomed and then faded for the generals, the Kaiser and the politicians. But when Russian mobilisation began, at the end of July, the German Schlieffen plan – founded on a quick victory over France in the west before moving troops east, to deal with Russia – demanded an immediate response. The Russians must not have time to shift huge forces to their western frontier.

The German High Command undoubtedly thought that victory would be easier in 1914 than later; the Social Democrats in the Reichstag were curbing military expenditure and the Russian army and economy were growing fast. Moltke wrote in a memorandum of July 28: "The military situation is thus becoming from day to day more unfavourable to us and may, if our prospective opponents go on preparing themselves at their leisure, lead to disastrous consequences for us." But on July 29 and 30, with war imminent, Bethmann-Hollweg drew back, wanting Austria-Hungary to negotiate with Serbia rather than spark what he called "a world conflagration".

On July 29, Britain's Foreign Secretary, Sir Edward Grey, tried to mediate, threatening Germany with British involvement. He also said he would do his best to secure "for Austria every possible satisfaction; there was no longer any question of a humiliating retreat for Austria, as the Serbs would in any case be punished and compelled, with the consent of Russia, to subordinate themselves to Austria's wishes". The Kaiser, told by his ambassador in London, Prince Lichnowsky – who was close to Grey – that

Britain would come to France's aid if war came, telegraphed the Tsar to beg him to delay Russia's general mobilisation. Nicholas II hesitated, then on the afternoon of July 30 was persuaded by his Foreign Minister, Sergey Sazonov, to let mobilisation go ahead. France was encouraging her Russian ally not to falter.

The confused events of late July do not suggest cool premeditation in Berlin. How hard it was to know what the Kaiser and his men might do next. Often they did not know themselves. In *The Sleepwalkers*, which became a best-seller in Germany, Christopher Clark wonders why more effort wasn't made to understand German fears and aspirations. Was it wrong to build up a navy when others in Europe were doing much the same? France and Russia, Clark argues, should have done more to curb Serbia.

A good deal of blame, as we have seen, can be attached to Austria-Hungary, which attacked Serbia after obtaining the "blank cheque" from Germany. But the "blank cheque" should never have been issued. In 1965 another German historian, Immanuel Geiss, came to Fischer's support, concluding that the war had its roots in Germany's *Weltpolitik*, or World Policy. "Germany was the aggressor… deliberately provoking Russia. [This] drove Russia, France and Britain to the wall and into a position when they could not but react against massive German ambitions." John Rohl, an expert on the Kaiser and his court, by and large reflects the modern consensus when he writes that there was "crucial evidence of intentionality on Germany's part".

CHAPTER SIX

WAS BRITAIN RIGHT TO JOIN IN?

Germany's leaders knew it was almost certain that Russia would intervene on Serbia's side if there was war in the Balkans. But Austria-Hungary had to be supported; Italy was unreliable; the Dual Monarchy was Germany's only real ally; the empire's disintegration would be a disaster that had to be prevented at all costs. And if there had to be war against Russia, as Berlin saw it, then better now than later.

Despite her huge army, Russia had been humiliatingly defeated by Japan in 1905 and was still recovering. The military hawks in Berlin, says Norman Stone, were "banging on the table: Germany could win a war now, but if she waited two or three years, Russia would be too strong". While her army seemed terrifyingly large, what "caused panic" was the growth of her railways. "Railways won wars." Everything depended on them. If one country moved fast in calling up and mobilising its soldiers, it could transport them by rail to an enemy's borders before the defending army was ready. Mobilisation was thus "like drawing a gun; whoever did so first enjoyed a huge strategic advantage". Some have compared the military set-up in Europe to a doomsday machine which, once started, would be impossible to stop.

Germany knew that Russia couldn't abandon Serbia and that France couldn't abandon Russia; for France to do that would be "to acquiesce in a German hegemony of Europe and her own reduction to the rank of a third-rate power". So Berlin was ready for war. But it was anxious not to be seen as the aggressor; it wanted Russia to make the first move, and, on July 30, its wish was granted. The Tsar, after much hesitation, ordered the mobilisation of Russia's armed forces. Not to do so, given Russia's administrative backwardness and the huge distances her reservists had to travel, would have put her at a huge disadvantage to the relatively small and efficient Germany.

So what of Britain? As an imperial power, Britain was unique. Lord Salisbury, the late 19th century prime minister, had talked of "splendid isolation"; of how Britain had no allies, only interests. Queen Victoria's diamond jubilee and her successors' coronations, with their obsequious Indian princes and troops mounted on camels and elephants, underlined the extent to which Britain's interests were global, rather than European.

But Britain was also Germany's great rival. In Michael Howard's view, Berlin was confused – in a state of what psychologists call "cognitive dissonance". Although France and Russia had to be defeated, Britain was the adversary "who must be faced down if Germany were to attain her rightful status as a World Power". Yet Britain had scarcely featured in Germany's war plans. These assumed that any expeditionary force Britain might send would be too small to make much difference, and that anyway the German navy could deal with the threat from Britain. But the German navy was in no position to deal with the Royal Navy; it was well behind in the naval arms race. So the German government was gambling on Britain's neutrality.

The British government in July 1914 was certainly distracted, grappling with the Home Rule crisis in Ulster, and Berlin was confident it wouldn't intervene.* The French ambassador in Berlin, Jules Cambon, warned the German foreign minister, Gottlieb von

BRITISH COMPLACENCY

"Are you afraid of invasion?" a German asks the narrator in a short story by Katherine Mansfield published in 1911. "You have no army. You should be." H.G. Wells in his 1916 novel *Mr Britling Sees It Through* imagines a young German's view of England on the eve of war. The country is pleasant but not serious; informal and quite chaotic. "Intimations of the future" came from a rebellious Ireland, from memories of Boer war defeats, from an uneasy India and the empire, from industrial unrest, from violent suffragettes. Meanwhile the British, like "everlasting children", played on. After all, why should prosperous Britons be anxious?

On leaving Oxford in 1913, the young historian Llewellyn Woodward was in Germany on a European tour, at a hotel in the Black Forest, when Archduke Franz Ferdinand was shot in Sarajevo. Other guests (including several Russians) thought it meant a war that would involve Britain.

To Woodward, the murders appeared to be just another Balkan incident that might have come from the best-selling novel, *The Prisoner of Zenda*.

Back in Oxford, at dinner in St John's College, the assassinations were scarcely mentioned and Woodward felt unable to mention the fear that he'd sensed in the Black Forest hotel. "It would have seemed ridiculous to suggest at dessert on this quiet Sunday evening that a European war might break out in a fortnight." He remembered later that undergraduates didn't concern themselves much with foreign affairs, preferring social questions and religion.

Jagow, that Berlin was wrong: this time Britain would not remain neutral in a European war, as she had in 1870. But Jagow shrugged: "you have your information and we have ours, which is completely different. We are confident of British neutrality."

The historian Vernon Bogdanor has claimed that the Central Powers might have hesitated if Britain had introduced conscription before 1914, thus building up an army to match those on the Continent. Then an Anglo-French alliance would have been formidable. But conscription under Prime Minister Herbert Asquith was inconceivable. Apart from Liberal opposition, the Treasury could not have coped. The cabinet was introducing measures of social reform and an early welfare state, modest compared with what Bismarck had already done for Germany, but expensive nonetheless.

To most Oxford professors, Woodward thought, Europe meant "the mountains of Switzerland, the cathedrals of France and ancient monuments of Greece and Italy" – not murders in Belgrade or fury in Bulgaria. Modern History was taught up to 1880 but "in fact no one bothered much about anything that happened after Waterloo". Oxford had "an extraordinary sense of security". Geoffrey Keynes, brother of the economist Maynard, thought the same about Cambridge. He believed that such a delightful feeling was impossible for later generations to imagine.

Britain wasn't just Oxford and Cambridge, of course. But, despite industrial unrest, rioting suffragettes, and bombs and rent strikes in Ireland, there was a widespread sense of stability. "In spite of the sporadic disorders up and down the land," wrote the social historian, Robert Roberts, who grew up in a Salford slum, the strikes and lock-outs, the syndicalist talk and "revolutionary situations", the undermass remained stable. Ignorant, unorganised, schooled in humility, they had neither the wit nor the will to revolt. Like the working class as a whole they went on gazing up still to the ineffable reaches of the middle and upper orders and felt that there stood wealth, wisdom and an ordained capacity for command far beyond a simple man's knowing, and that leadership they would follow.
It took the worst war in history to disenchant them.

Amongst Britain's ruling class there was little appetite for war. The British ambassador in Paris, Sir Francis Bertie, wrote on July 27: "It seems incredible that the Russian Government should plunge Europe into war in order to make themselves the protectors of the Serbians." Did it really make sense for Britain to risk everything to save a troublesome Balkan state?

Nor was there much fondness in Britain (particularly among liberals) for Serbia's protector, Russia. In many quarters, war between Germany and Britain was almost unthinkable. "Germany, the model country, with the largest Social Democrat party, the best local government, the best education in Europe. Why go to war with her at the side of Tsarist Russia?"

The Foreign Secretary, Sir Edward Grey, and the War Minister, Lord Haldane, might argue the importance of preserving the balance of power but the prevailing view was firmly against intervention. "Had Germany not invaded Belgium, it is an open question whether Britain would have maintained her neutrality," says Michael Howard. It was the German invasion of Belgium which changed everything.

The fortifications on the short Franco-German border were so strong that a direct German attack on France was all but impossible. Instead the army followed the so-called Schlieffen Plan, a plan of attack devised by Moltke's predecessor as Chief of Staff, General Schlieffen, whereby Germany would deal with France by invading her through neutral Belgium, before turning to Russia.

So on August 2 Germany demanded that the Belgian monarch, King Albert, give her armies right of passage through his country. The demand was rejected. Two days later Germany invaded Belgium, and Britain declared war on Germany.

British public opinion, until this point divided, was divided no longer. Belgium's independence had been guaranteed by a treaty in 1839. Now the Germans were violating it. There was a strong emotional reaction to this bullying of a small nation. Without the invasion, the British Empire might have remained on the sidelines, an uneasy observer of a war which Germany would probably have won.

It is a historical irony that "gallant little Belgium" was no paragon; indeed her "deplorable record of inhumanity as the colonial power in the Congo was surpassed only by that of Germany in South-West Africa". But in modern history larger democracies have tended to see it as a moral duty to protect smaller ones from having their sovereignty violated. If Germany had managed to avoid seeming the aggressor against Russia (which mobilised first), she was clearly the aggressor now.

Sir Edward Grey has been depicted as limited and insular, ignorant of foreign languages, obsessed with fishing and watching birds. He has been criticised for not making it plain early on that Britain would take the side of France and Russia in any war. There was too much doubt, his critics claim. A country's foreign policy should be clear, and Britain's wasn't.

But this ignores the realities of democratic politics: parliament was divided, and there was no formal guarantee to France or Russia. It's also unfair to Grey who, as Gary Sheffield says, had worked "strenuously" for peace, having proposed an international conference or mediation on no less than six occasions during the July crisis. But the atmosphere had changed. Germany, which had given its ally Austria-Hungary a "blank cheque" to do what she pleased against Serbia, refused to attend, feeling that she would be isolated as the

Hapsburg Empire's only defender.

A popular view in Britain has always been that while World War Two was a "good" war, fought against a clearly evil regime, World War One was a "bad" one, not worth fighting. So would neutrality in 1914 have been a better option? The German Chancellor, Bethmann-Hollweg, expressed amazement to the British ambassador in Berlin: "Just for a scrap of paper (the 1839 treaty with Belgium) Great Britain was going to make war on a kindred nation who desired nothing better than to be friends with her."

Yet little more than a month after the war began, on September 9, Bethmann-Hollweg drafted a list of demands which reflected Berlin's determination to dominate continental Europe. "The aim of the war," he wrote, "is to provide us with [security] guarantees, from east to west, for the foreseeable future, through the enfeeblement of our adversaries." Belgium and Holland were to be transformed into vassal states. Russia's borders would be shrunk. A vast German colonial empire would be created in central Africa.

It is true that this was a personal list, written after the outbreak of war. But would German ambitions have been less aggressive if Britain had kept out? The historian Niall Ferguson, in *The Pity of War*, argues that Britain's intervention in 1914 was "nothing less than the greatest error in modern history". Germany, he says, did not pose an essential threat to British interests; the build-up of the German navy was exaggerated and was in any case partly defensive. It was the British government "which ultimately decided to turn a continental war into a world war, a conflict which lasted twice as long and cost many more lives" than it would have if Britain had not stepped in.

Ferguson is convinced that the peace which Germany would have imposed on Europe is one with which Britain "with her maritime empire, could… have lived". The Europe that would have emerged from a German victory would have been quite benign, "not wholly unlike the [Austria-Hungary] European Union we know today". Ferguson concludes that "it would have been infinitely preferable if Germany could have achieved its hegemonic position on the continent without two world wars".

A theoretical argument like this is hard to disprove; there is no way of testing its truth. Clearly Britain's tentative approach to European commitments, giving only provisional support to France and Russia, ended in failure. But what else could the government have done? Grey and some of his cabinet colleagues, such as Winston Churchill, believed in the case for war before Belgium was

ARGUING OVER THE CAUSES

In the 1920s, the American historian, Sydney Bradshaw Fay, argued that there were four main causes: nationalism, militarism, imperialism and, most importantly, the alliance system. In Fay's view the "greatest single underlying cause" was the competing alliance system: France, Russia, Britain on the one hand; Germany, Austria-Hungary and Italy on the other.

Revisionist historians question his view. Far from being too strong the alliances formed can just as easily be seen as too weak; Germany, unable to count on Italy, felt insecure. Frank McDonough argued that "a fundamental problem which contributed to the outbreak of war was the lack of a fully effective balance of power in Europe – not its existence". (Sheffield, p11)

Another long-standing theory revisionist historians now tend to discount is that the war was caused by an arms race. David Stevenson, among others, has argued that

a "self-reinforcing cycle of heightened preparedness... was an essential element in the conjuncture that led to disaster..." Yet, as Niall Ferguson says, not all arms races end in conflict, the Cold War being a good example. A variation on the arms race theory is the idea that Europe slithered into war in 1914, as implied in the title of Christopher Clark's The Sleepwalkers. "The statesmen were overwhelmed by the magnitude of events," wrote A.J.P. Taylor. No one wanted war but the logistics of mobilisation meant you had to be there before your opponent or risk defeat: war was the consequence.

Most modern historians are unconvinced by the war-by-accident theory: the leaders of the great powers cannot be so easily excused. They all pursued what they thought were logical objectives. In their own eyes at least, they were perfectly rational.

invaded. Their view, however, did not reflect domestic political opinion. It is unlikely they that they would have carried their point without the invasion.

Nor does Germany's behaviour in Belgium and northern France in the early months of the war support Ferguson's sanguine view; the German army murdered thousands of Belgian and French people of all ages in "a systematic attempt to impose its will, show its might and suppress imaginary guerrilla resistance". In his war memoirs, published in the 1930s, David Lloyd George, who succeeded Asquith as British prime minister, argued that the war had been a tragic accident. Nobody wanted it but "nations backed their machines over the precipice". Christopher Clark, in *The Sleep-walkers*, takes the same line:

> The outbreak of war in 1914 was not an Agatha Christie drama at the end of which we will discover the culprit standing over a corpse in the conservatory with a smoking pistol. There is no smoking gun in the story; or, rather, there is one in the hands of every major character. Viewed in this light, the outbreak of war was a tragedy, not a crime.

Most modern historians reject this view. Overwhelmingly they believe that there was a smoking gun – in the hands of both Austria-Hungary and Germany, with the greatest share of the blame attached to Germany, which could have restrained its unwieldy and anxious ally. Britain was morally bound to join in.

The trouble is that by 1914 "no one trusted the Germans", says Norman Stone; Lloyd George, "the brightest figure in British politics", thought that a Germany controlling the resources of Russia would be unbeatable. Ferguson's "Panglossian view" of a "Kaiser's European Union", says Gary Sheffield, has rightly not achieved "much acceptance"; the consequences of a German victory would have been "cataclysmic" for Britain. After defeating France and Russia, would Germany really have been content to accommodate Britain, or to acquiesce in its mastery of the seas? It seems unlikely.

SIR EDWARD GREY

The person responsible for Britain's foreign policy was described by the Kaiser as "a capable sort of country gentleman". For once, says Margaret Macmillan, the Kaiser was not far wrong.

Educated at Winchester and Balliol College, Oxford, Grey was hardly an obvious choice as Foreign Secretary. He had no interest in travel, "unless it was to go shooting and fishing in Scotland", and while in office only visited the Continent once, in 1914, as part of a royal visit to Paris.

As a young man, Grey inherited an estate in the north-east of England to which he and his wife, Dorothy escaped as often as possible, living simply with one servant, taking particular pleasure in the red squirrels: these "little red fellows continued to comfort him all his life long ", says his biographer. His wife loved him but abhorred sex, and Grey, "ever the gentleman", agreed early in their marriage that they should live together as brother and sister. His life had its share of tragedy. In 1906, Dorothy was thrown from a pony cart and died from her injuries; five years later Grey's beloved brother George was killed by a lion in Africa.

This strange, rather lonely figure did more than anyone else to ensure Britain's participation in a war that he dreaded. After announcing in parliament that Britain couldn't stand aside, he retreated to his office. "I hate war... I hate war," he said, banging the table miserably. Later that same evening, looking out of his window into St James's Park, he made perhaps the most famous of all remarks about World War One: "The lamps are going out all over Europe; we shall not see them lit again in our life- time."

TEN FACTS
ABOUT WORLD WAR ONE

1. Anti-German feeling was so strong in Britain that, in 1917, George V was forced to change his surname from Saxe-Coburg-Gotha to Windsor.

2. It is widely thought that the first day of the Somme was the bloodiest of the conflict. This is not so. In August 1914 the French army paid an even more terrible daily cost, suffering more than a million casualties in the first five months of war, including 329,000 dead. The Germans had 800,000 casualties in the same period.

3. An estimated 16.5 million people died during the war. The influenza epidemic which followed it (possibly caused by the churning up of rich, microbe-laden soil in north France and Belgium) killed some 20 million more.

4. Both the British king, George V, and the Kaiser, Wilhelm II, were grandsons of Queen Victoria.

5. Britain was the only country to fight both world wars on the side of the allies from the first day to the last.

6. World War One was the catalyst for surgeon Harold Gillies to attempt facial reconstruction on many of the victims of shrapnel, laying the foundations for plastic

surgery as we know it today.

7. The loudest explosion in the war was made by the simultaneous detonation of 900,000 lbs of explosives in 19 underground tunnels at Messines Ridge in Belgium in 1917. The explosions were heard by Lloyd George in his Downing Street study, 140 miles away.

8. The most decorated private soldier was Henry Tandey, who won the VC for "conspicuous bravery and initiative" at the fifth battle of Ypres in 1918. It has been claimed that he could have shot Adolf Hitler, then a German soldier, but spared his life because he was wounded and unarmed. Hitler himself, at a meeting with Neville Chamberlain, the British prime minister, 20 years later, pointed at a picture of Tandey which hung in his (Hitler's) study and said: "That man came so near to killing me that I thought I should never see Germany again."

9. By the end of the war, around 114 million parcels and two billion letters had been delivered from Britain to the front line in France. The animal-loving fictional character Doctor Dolittle was created in the trenches: Hugh Lofting invented him in illustrated letters to his children.

10. On 24th December 1914, German troops in Ypres, Belgium, began to sing "Stille Nacht", and were joined by British troops from the other side of No Man's Land. Soon, messages were being shouted across, and an agreed ceasefire commenced for the duration of Christmas Day. This event became known as the "Christmas Truce".

PART TWO:

THE WAR

Archduke Franz Ferdinand of Austria (1863 - 1914)

CHAPTER SEVEN

THE SCHLIEFFEN PLAN

In the late 1890s, Jan Bloch wrote a six-volume work called *Is War Possible?* Bloch was a Wilhelm II businessman who had studied recent wars, particularly the Franco-Prussian war of 1870. He believed that if victory for one side did not come quickly – as it had for the Prussians – modern firepower and defensive strength must make for a long and terrible conflict.

> Everybody will be entrenched in the next war...
> The spade will be as indispensable as the rifle. The first
> thing every man will have to do, if he cares for his life at
> all, will be to dig a hole in the ground. War, instead of
> being a hand-to-hand contest in which the combatants
> measure their physical and moral superiority, will

become a kind of stalemate.

Bloch also foresaw the effectiveness of the Allied naval blockade which led to food shortages and famine in Germany. The hardships suffered by civilians would lead to the revolutions which European leaders constantly feared.

Bloch's work was extraordinarily prophetic, foretelling the course and outcome of the First World War. So why wasn't more notice taken of it at the time? One answer is that two wars fought shortly after his predictions (Britain against the Boers in South Africa in 1899-1902 and Japan against Russia in 1905) showed that "although the new weapons certainly inflicted terrible losses, decisive battles could still be fought and won". The lesson European armies drew from these wars was that it was still possible to win if your soldiers were brave and armed with up-to-date weapons.

But another lesson was learnt, too – that victory, as Bloch argued, had to come quickly. Japan had nearly bankrupted herself in defeating Russia; Russia's defeat had caused a revolution. Perhaps the Europeans should have paid more attention to the American civil war, fought in the 1860s, which had been long and bloody.

In 1914, the assumption on all sides was that the war would be short. Britain, like Germany, was hugely dependent on foreign trade. How could her economy possibly survive a long war? Sir Felix Schuster, chairman of the bankers' association, "assured everyone that [it] would have to be stopped after six months". The Hungarian finance minister, asked how long he could pay for the conflict, replied: three weeks. In the armies which went to war it was believed that it would all be over before Christmas. The Russian High Command, asking for new typewriters, were told that the fighting would not last long enough to justify the expense. "No war has ever begun with such a fundamental misunderstanding of its nature," says Norman Stone.

The Schlieffen Plan, the basis for Germany's strategy, was originally devised by Field-Marshal Alfred von Schlieffen, the Chief of the German General Staff from 1892 until 1906. The plan envisaged a massive offensive intended to knock France out of the war in six weeks. The military historian John Keegan has called the Schlieffen Plan "the most important government document written in any country in the first decade of the twentieth century".

Schlieffen believed in the primacy of force. He was a man with no hobbies and a passion for war plans who was often at his desk by 6 a.m, after a ride in the great Berlin park, the Tiergarten. A member of Schlieffen's staff once heard the doorbell of his Berlin apartment ring on Christmas Eve. It was a courier with a "Christmas present" from the General: a military exercise requiring a detailed appraisal by the evening of Christmas Day. The same aide, when on a train journey with Schlieffen in East Prussia, broke the grim silence by commenting on the beauty of a river, to be told that it was "an insignificant obstacle" to an attack. The Chief of the General Staff was always on duty (though sometimes, late in the evening, he would "relax" by reading military history to his daughters).

Inspired by Hannibal's crushing victory over the Roman legions at Cannae in 216 BC, Schlieffen decided that in the event of war there must first be an overwhelming offensive against France; Russia, which would be slower to mobilise, could be dealt with afterwards. Because of the French fortresses along the short Austria-Hungary frontier, the offensive, involving seven eighths of Germany's strength, "must not shrink from violating the neutrality of Belgium and Luxembourg ".

Schlieffen's plan, developed during the 1890s, was unveiled in a Grand Memorandum of 1905, then refined by his successor, Helmut von Moltke. The General Staff had calculated that the French Army must be crushed in six weeks if they were to have time to move enough divisions east to counter the threat from Russia. The great outflanking movement envisaged by Schlieffen was aimed at "surrounding and annihilating" the French armies in a *Schlacht ohne Morgen* – 'a battle without a tomorrow'. Moltke had adapted the plan to avoid invading Holland, for if the war dragged on a neutral Holland would be vital for Germany's economy.

The German army in 1914 was not as strong as Schlieffen had hoped it would be. But it was better prepared than the French army. The French lacked the heavy artillery available to the Germans – their own "having been stuffed into fortresses". They were also short of two other weapons which served the Germans well: the light mortars which could hurl shells behind fortifications or among trees, and the spades, or "entrenching tools", which enabled soldiers to dig holes in the ground, making them difficult to spot and almost invulnerable except to heavy shelling.

The fortresses of northern France and Belgium, although elaborate and heavily armed, proved wholly inadequate against the German heavy artillery which could deliver high explosive at a range of ten miles. Liège, on Germany's border with Belgium, lasted just two days. By mid August the three German armies (three quarters of a million men, in 52 divisions) were moving with great speed across Belgium, covering 20 miles a day, an amazing achievement. They drove before them thousands of refugees, clogging the roads, and treated those who remained behind with a harshness intended to discourage resistance. An estimated 5,000 Belgian civilians were shot during the march through the country and buildings were set indiscriminately on fire.[*]

Meanwhile, France's commander-in-chief, General Joseph Joffre, was preoccupied with his own offensive, launched initially into German-occupied Alsace-Lorraine further south. In their highly visible blue coats and red trousers, the French army suffered dreadful casualties. They endured heavy losses to the north, too, as the German advance swept forward, its heavy artillery often destroying French units before their lighter guns could be

---

[*] These terror tactics had been a vital part of Schlieffen's plan. Moltke, more optimistic, had apparently hoped that the Belgians might cheer and salute the invaders.

GERMAN ATROCITIES

In 1914, Louvain in Belgium was a "beautiful and civilised little town" with a university library containing some 200,000 books; classics, works of theology, a small collection of songs written down by a monk in the ninth century and illuminated manuscripts over which monks had toiled for years. (Macmillan, pXVII) On August 25th, German troops arrived; shots were fired, probably by drunken or nervous German soldiers; other German soldiers, however, unnerved by the gunfire, and convinced they were under attack, began reprisals. The mayor, the head of the university and several police officers were shot. Eventually 250 out of the town's 100,000 population were dead, many more beaten up.

Around midnight on August 25th German soldiers went to the library "and poured petrol about". (Macmillan, pXIX) By morning the building had been consumed by fire. The precious collection of books was gone. "The centre of the city is a smoking heap of ruins," said a professor. "Everybody has fled; at the windows of cellars I see frightened faces." Louvain was just the beginning. Shortly afterwards, Rheims Cathedral, where most French kings had been crowned, was pulverised by German guns. "This was only the start as Europe laid waste to itself," says Margaret Macmillan.

brought to bear. With the French army falling back, the two corps of the British Expeditionary Force, sent over the Channel to help, barely had time to take up their positions before they were under fire. French and British forces were forced into a long, hot retreat which lasted for two weeks.

Then, at the beginning of September, came the Battle of the Marne: the allies counter-attacked; the Schlieffen Plan fell apart, and with it Germany's entire war strategy.

The Schlieffen Plan was always likely to fail if Belgium decided to fight and the British government honoured its 1839 pledge to defend her. The reversal of German fortunes in early September can thus be attributed primarily to what has been called "the vast fallacy of Schlieffen". By early September the plan was coming unstuck: it required "millions of men, many of them newly recalled from soft civilian life, to march vast distances across western Europe carrying heavy loads in summer heat". The problem, as Roger Chickering writes, was that the plan was "geared to the wrong century". The Battle of the Marne (September 5 to 12, 1914) not only halted the German advance on Paris; it effectively ended Germany's hopes of winning the war. Berlin was now faced with the almost impossible task of fighting a long war on two fronts, east and west. There have been endless arguments about who deserves most credit for the victory: famously, Joffre said that he did not know who won it, but he knew who would have been blamed if it had been lost.

The German marching columns lost cohesion. Moltke's leadership was erratic and the German commander-in-chief also faced the huge technical problem of controlling six German armies, all fighting on foreign soil. France's defeats and her retreat at least enabled General Joffre to exploit the communications systems of his own country to his advantage.

When General Alexander von Kluck swung the German First Army to the east of Paris, Joffre halted the retreat of his main force and launched a counter-offensive from the capital against von Kluck's flank. So important was the need to move troops quickly at the beginning of the battle that some of them were ferried from Paris to the front by taxi, "a great patriotic legend", says Norman Stone, "though the taxis kept their meters running".

British forces joined the battle. Between September 9 and 11, the Germans were forced to fall back to the river Aisne, digging themselves in on a chalk ridge rising 500 feet above the river, and fortifying their positions with barbed wire. Further Allied attacks were unsuccessful. Moltke, 150 miles behind the front in Luxembourg, struggled to deal with the battle – he was not even involved in the decision to withdraw. Joffre, on the other hand, had used the French railways effectively to move his troops, his dynamic generalship contrasting with Moltke's hesitancy. After the battle Moltke had a nervous breakdown and was replaced by the more

ITALY

Italy, to the fury of its Triple Alliance partners, stayed neutral in 1914. Then, in May 1915, it declared war on Austria-Hungary, having been promised under a secret treaty with the Allies all Italian- speaking regions south of the Alps, along with South Tyrol and parts of Slovenia and Dalmatia. Its treachery to its former allies confirmed, in the view of Conrad von Hötzendorf, that "it was a snake whose head had not been crushed in time".

There followed two years of terrible fighting in the mountains and passes of the Dolomites, where incompetent and cruel Italian generalship suffering of poorly led troops. At the peace treaty Italy, as one of the victorious allies, gained territory in the north but was disappointed not to get what she'd been promised in the Balkans, much of which went to the new Yugoslavia.

vigorous General Eric von Falkenhayn.

When the war was over the German army claimed it had been "stabbed in the back" – that the war had been lost because of the collapse of the home front. According to this argument, says Hew Strachan, "the army itself had been undefeated in the field. But such assertions ignored the events of 1914. France had been saved. To many, Marne was a miracle and Joffre a new Napoleon." Nonetheless, by mid September both armies were temporarily exhausted. And by the end of the month they were dug in at the beginning of what became a stalemate that was to last nearly four years. Jan Bloch's gloomy prediction was to prove all too true.

British soldiers lined up in a narrow trench in 1915, on the southern section of the Gallipoli peninsula

DOUGLAS HAIG

Douglas Haig, one of the most controversial figures in British military history, took over from Sir John French as C-in-C of the British Expeditionary Force in December 1915. The scion of a Scottish whisky-distilling family, who passed out top in his year at Sandhurst, Haig's reputation suffered after the war with the publication of his diaries, which exposed apparent callousness in the face of the suffering on the western front.

"He seemed to move through the horrors... as if guided by some inner voice," says the military historian John Keegan.

As a young officer he had taken to attending séances, where a medium put him in touch with Napoleon: as Commander-in-Chief he fell under the influence of a Presbyterian chaplain whose sermons confirmed him in his belief that he was in direct communication with God... (Keegan, p311)

Despite his strangeness, Haig was an efficient soldier; his preparations for the Somme were typically thorough. His critics blame him for this dreadful battle, what Keegan calls Britain's "greatest military tragedy of the twentieth century, indeed of their national military history". (Keegan p321) Haig's detractors point to the ineffective artillery bombardment and, most of all, to his decision to press on relentlessly in spite of the horrific casualties.

Haig was also attacked by Lloyd George, for, among other things, his distance from the front line and the relative luxury of his chateau HQ near

Amiens. "The distance between the chateaux and the dugouts was as great as that from the fixed stars to the caverns of the earth." (John Terraine, Douglas Haig, p171)

In 1963, the military historian John Terraine came to his defence, arguing that he had been unfairly demonised; in the circumstances he did the best he could; he had little choice but to wage a war of attrition. Such a view is more in line with modern revisionism, which holds that while none of Britain's generals were outstanding in World War One, Haig was abler than caricature allows. He deserves credit for the final Allied offensive in 1918 which showed that he had learnt the lessons of earlier battles.

General Schlieffen in 1906, the same year that he devised the infamous plan

CHAPTER EIGHT

LIONS LED BY DONKEYS

T. E. Lawrence memorably said of the British Army in World War One that "the men were often gallant fighters, but the generals as often gave away in stupidity what they had gained in ignorance". His derision has been echoed by countless writers and military strategists. British generals, it was said, had "a captious and jealous rigidity of outlook, a purblind psychology... as a consequence of their narrow education". Max Hastings is not exaggerating when he says that no warrior tribe in history "has received such mockery and contempt from posterity as have been heaped upon Britain's commanders of the First World War".

One reason for the mockery is that while warriors in history have tended to be stoical and often inarticulate, World War One was chronicled by many highly literate citizen soldiers, especially poets, who conveyed the horrors and, as many of them saw it, futility of the conflict in a way unmatched before or since. Very little great poetry emerged from World War Two. Siegfried Sassoon wrote memorably of Britain's commanders in the trenches:

"Good morning, good morning!" the General said
When we met him last week on our way to the line.
Now the soldiers he smiled at are most of 'em dead,
And we're cursing his staff for incompetent swine.
"He's a cheery old card," grunted Harry to Jack,
As they slogged up to Arras with rifle and pack.
But he did for them both with his plan of attack.

More than 40 years later the likes of Sir John French, Commander-in-Chief of the wartime British Expeditionary Force on the Western Front, and Douglas Haig, his successor, were caricatured in Alan Clark's entertaining but unscholarly 1961 book, *The Donkeys*, with its famous description of British troops as "lions led by donkeys". Clark later admitted that he had made up the quote, attributed to the Kaiser. But his analysis suited the spirit of a time when there was strong feeling, after years of Conservative government, against Britain's supposedly class-bound and out-of-date establishment.

It inspired the 1963 musical, *Oh What A Lovely War!* and later satirical depictions of World War One generals as in the BBC TV series, *Blackadder*.

Some writers continue to dismiss Britain's World War One

generals as, in the words of John Laffan, Blimpish "butchers and bunglers". Most, though, take a more sympathetic view. A.J.P. Taylor says that "the war was beyond the capacity of generals and statesmen alike". John Terraine argues that there could have been no swift victory on the Western Front and that the British generals, Douglas Haig in particular, did a pretty good job.

It is certainly true that the British Expeditionary Force, when it went to France, was lamentably under-equipped and under-trained. Unlike the German army, it was not designed for continental war and, until conscription in 1916, was made up entirely of volunteers. After that the problem was that the new troops were not professionals but men who had to be rushed through training to face a German conscript army with far more experience. Haig recalled in June 1919: "we went into this war lacking preparation for it… Throughout the whole process… we were making desperate efforts to catch up." The historian Peter Simkins has written that

> [Herbert] Asquith's Liberal government had committed Britain to a major industrialised war… without providing the means – or even a clear blueprint for further action – with which to conduct and fight such a war.

As Simkins says, it is wholly wrong to put all the blame for this on the generals.

This is especially true given that it was the politicians at home who ultimately controlled Britain's armies and strategy. Take the decision to mount a huge offensive at the Somme. Haig wanted the attack to be in Flanders, closer to supplies and strategic targets such as ports and coalmines. But Asquith's government bowed to pressure from the French, who wanted to attack at exactly the point where the French and British armies met in the trench line. This happened also to be where the Germans were especially well dug in, contributing greatly to the mass slaughter that followed.

In the immediate aftermath of the conflict most of the soldiers who returned from the Western Front were not disposed to blame their generals, though there was anger about the inefficient handling of demobilisation, which led to strikes and mutinies.

It was not until the end of the 1920s, when the Depression began, that the mood changed, and books such as Robert Graves's *Good-bye to All That*, Eric Maria *Remarque's All Quiet on the Western Front* and Siegfried Sassoon's *Memoirs of a Fox-hunting Man* began to paint a different picture of Britain's military leadership. It was this mood that led to the hugely popular Peace Movement of the 1930s, and to the removal of allied generals, previously catalogued as "The Men Who Won the War", from Madame Tussaud's waxwork gallery in London. In 1933, a motion in an Oxford Union debate was carried by 275 votes to 153 "that this House will in no circumstances fight for King and Country".

Among those who encouraged the belief that the British war effort was ineptly run was Captain Basil Liddell Hart. Briefly a soldier on the Western Front, he became a pundit on military affairs, publishing a book in 1930 which denounced the myopia of Britain's generals and their failure to exploit technology, above all the tank, soon enough. Liddell Hart, whose views won approval from important figures of the day, including Winston Churchill and Lloyd George, helped to entrench the idea that the generals were unimaginative and could have secured victory at a vastly smaller cost.

C.S. Forester was much influenced by Liddell Hart's views when he wrote his brilliant World War One novel, *The General*. He likened the generals to "a group of savages" debating

> how to extract a screw from a piece of wood. Accustomed only to nails, they had made one effort to pull out the screw by main force, and now that it had failed they were devising methods of applying more force still.

Among the novel's admirers was Adolf Hitler, who gave specially bound copies to key subordinates, telling them that it "offered a penetrating study of the British military caste they would soon meet and defeat in battle".

Modern scholars, however, have pointed out that Forester's analogy of extracting a screw by force is flawed; at the time when the war was fought there simply didn't exist a better method of extracting screws – there was no cheaper, swifter route to victory. The tank (which Churchill championed) was simply not at the disposal of either side for most of the war. "The Western Front's dominant reality was that the available means of defence proved more effectual than the means of attack."

On the occasions when a breakthrough was achieved neither side had the necessary mobility to take proper advantage of it. Even in World War Two, Liddell Hart's belief in the "indirect approach", in victory through manoeuvre, only proved possible when defenders suffered "a moral collapse", like the French in 1940, the Italians in 1941 and the Russians during the first months of Hitler's invasion. When a defending army fought with staunchness, as the

Wehrmacht almost always did, Liddell Hart was shown to be quite wrong.

One reason the British suffered relatively high casualties compared with the Germans was that, unlike the Germans (or the Turks in Gallipoli), they had to attack. In the mud of the Western Front, against trenches and barbed wire, attacks were nightmarishly difficult. In J.G. Fuller's words, "it was the bullet, spade and wire which were the enemy on every front".

The other problem was the difficulty of communication. Defenders knew their ground well, had laid down telephone lines and could receive information and take decisions more quickly. Richard Holmes writes:

> It was always easier for the defender, driven back on his own communications, to reinforce his failure than it was for an attacker, his communications stretched across the abrasive edge of a battlefield, to reinforce his success.

The defenders were also closer to their railway and road systems, so they could rush reinforcements in where they were needed. At Loos in 1915, the Germans managed to quadruple their reserves from 4,000 to 16,000 in two days. And it was only in 1918 that the Allied armies got the sophisticated signal services and proper wireless sets that enabled them to counterbalance their disadvantage as attackers.

So why – a question frequently asked – did the Allies keep attacking? The answer is: what else could they do? To remain in their trenches would have been to acquiesce in enemy occupation of a large swathe of Belgium and France. The Germans, unlike the Allies, could concede a little territory if it was tactically expedient to do so; for the French, it was unthinkable to give up more of their soil.

What has been called "the exigencies of coalition warfare" added to the pressure. How long would the Russians hold out in the east? What would happen if they lost? The Russians endured horrendous losses on the eastern front and continuing pressure in the west seemed essential if they were to be kept in the war at all. A

WAR IN THE MIDDLE EAST

Unstable for many years, the 400-year-old Ottoman Empire (now Turkey) was still the greatest independent Islamic power in the world. The war widened when she came in on the side of Germany and Austria-Hungary in November 1914, declaring jihad (holy war) against France, Russia and Britain.

Both sides had courted the Sultan, but the Ottomans were most impressed with the industrial and military power of Germany. They saw war as the opportunity to regain lost territories, to re-confirm their imperial glory after a series of setbacks in Libya and the Balkans, and above all to get revenge on an old enemy, Russia. A key war aim was "the destruction of our Muscovite enemy to obtain a natural frontier to our empire, which should include and unite all branches of our race".

The Allies, looking for an alternative to the stalemate on the Western Front, tried early in 1915 to capture Istanbul and knock Turkey out of the war. After a naval offensive failed, a new plan was tried: landing an expeditionary force on the Gallipoli peninsula. This disastrous strategy, the brainchild of Winston Churchill, resulted in the deaths of 250,000 Allied troops. Further humiliation came in 1916 when an Anglo-Indian force under General Charles Townshend surrendered to the Ottomans at Kut-el-Amara, 100 miles south of Baghdad.

Britain redoubled its efforts and regained the initiative under General Sir Edmund Allenby, who captured Jerusalem in December 1917, becoming the holy city's first Christian conqueror since the Crusades. In 1918, assisted by Arab allies and T.E. Lawrence ("Lawrence of Arabia"), Allenby broke the Ottoman armies, capturing Damascus and Aleppo. The war ended with the British occupying vast swathes of the Middle East.

After the war, the Ottoman Middle East was parcelled out among the Allies, aided by ambitious local rulers such as Emir Feisal of Mecca. Jordan, Iraq and Palestine came under British control; the French took what are now Lebanon and Syria. The British had already promised support for a Jewish homeland in Palestine in the Balfour Declaration of 1917, if (the text optimistically said) the rights of the local Arabs were not affected. The settlement fostered an instability and tension between local powers and external interests that continues to be a source of conflict today.

major reason why the premature offensives of 1915 seemed necessary is that, in Lord Kitchener's words, it was "doubtful how much longer [the Russian army] could withstand the German blows".

The arguments in defence of the generals, however, can be pushed too far. Britain's top brass cannot be blamed for the logistical problems: the lack of powerful guns and adequate stocks of shells, or the fact many of the shells the army did have didn't explode.

But British commanders made tactical mistakes: they persisted – as at the Somme in 1916 and Passchendaele in 1917 – in using long, heavy bombardments, churning up the ground and eliminating any element of surprise without actually destroying the German front line. They kept campaigns going well after it was clear that they were a failure, unnecessarily wasting lives at the Somme, Ypres and Passchendaele. And there is much truth in Niall Ferguson's claim that "the entire culture of the British regular army militated against effective improvisation". The command structure was too rigid, and there was a lack of flexibility that undoubtedly cost lives.

Were Britain's generals any worse than their predecessors, or successors? In the second half of World War Two, Britain won some victories under the leadership of competent, if not inspired, commanders. But it is difficult to show that the British commanders of the early World War Two years displayed higher skills than those of Sir John French and Douglas Haig. And contrary to the myth that Britain's Great War generals avoided the worst of the front line, they were perhaps "too eager to get away from their desks", in the words of a staff officer. Between 1914 and 1918, 34 were killed by artillery and 22 by small arms fire; in

An early model British Mark I "male" tank, named C-15, near Thiepval, September 25th 1916

World War Two, a total of 21 generals were killed in action.

It is also a myth that World War One was a uniquely awful war. World War Two was much more costly in terms of lives; far bloodier attritional clashes were necessary to defeat Nazism. The British, however, were spared these. The killing fields of 1941-45 were not on the Somme or at Verdun in western Europe. They were in the east, with the Russians (who inflicted an extraordinary 92% of the German army's total casualties) suffering 27 million dead. The World War Two generals "were spared the odium of presiding over bloodbaths comparable with those of 1914-18 not by their own genius, but because the Russians did most of the killing and dying ".

CHAPTER NINE

PROVOKING AMERICA

It is extraordinary that the United States should have fought in the First World War. Most of those involved in the vast immigration into America during the 19th and early 20th centuries had come to escape European poverty and persecution: Jews beaten by the Tsar's Cossacks, Irish starved in the potato famine, Germans wanting a better life than under feudalism or urban poverty.

Why should any of these people take up arms in support of King George V or the Emperors of Germany and Russia? Were the Allies any better than the Central Powers? The Irish had a particular dislike for the British; the Jews and the Poles loathed the Russians; and the large German community, strong in the midwest, had no wish to fight against their old homeland. To many

Americans, Europe's self-destruction showed how wise they'd been to leave it.

Their president in 1914, Woodrow Wilson, told them that the country would keep out of the war. A self-righteous Presbyterian, previously head of Princeton University, Wilson was by inclination a man of peace, and he wanted to carry through domestic reforms that would be much harder to achieve under wartime conditions.

Wilson thought that the United States had "nothing to do" with the war whose causes, he said, "cannot touch us". However, there were strong American cultural ties with Britain, especially among the powerful WASP east coast establishment. There was also American sympathy for France, the old ally from the War of Independence, and shock at the German invasion of neutral Belgium. (Russian atrocities in the German province of East Prussia, which the Tsar's forces invaded in August 1914, attracted little attention.)

Pressure groups formed to argue the case for and against the war. These ranged from the pacifist "American Union Against Militarism" to the "Preparedness Movement" – backed by business, retired senior officers and the Anglophile east coast elite – which called for stronger armed forces and intervention abroad.

The Anglophile case was fuelled by anxiety about Germany's aggressive intentions towards areas of US interest such as the Far East and Central and South America. Wilson's closest adviser, Colonel House, favoured the Allies, and although the Secretary of State, William Jennings Bryan – a mid-western isolationist – did not, the dominant view in Washington, from early on, was against Germany.

US trade with the Allies soared, easily outstripping that with the Central Powers of Germany and Austria-Hungary; US banks had made far greater loans to France and Britain than to other belligerents. While the British blockade, imposed on Britain's enemies by the Royal Navy, threatened US exports, President Wilson – encouraged by his Anglophile ambassador in London, Walter Page – tolerated this, thereby showing early favour to the Allies.

His stance hardened in February 1915 when the Germans declared an unrestricted submarine war on shipping in the waters round Britain; this meant no longer following "cruiser rules", the convention under which ships were checked before being sunk, with the submarine surfacing first, inspecting the vessel and when appropriate giving the crew time to take to the lifeboats. Sinking ships on sight was thought to be barbaric, and the Allies stepped up their propaganda about German "brutality".

Then, in March 1915, the British steamship Falaba was sunk by a German U boat, with one American among those drowned. Worse came on May 7 1915 with the sinking of the British passenger liner Lusitania by the German submarine U-20. The German government had announced in the American press that passengers travelling in vessels carrying exports to Britain or France would put themselves in danger of U Boat attacks. The German submarine fleet was the world's biggest so the threat was serious – and the Lusitania had arms for Britain in her hold.

Struck by a torpedo, she went down off the Irish coast, and among the 1,201 who died were 128 Americans, and many women and children. In the context of war the German action may have been defensible, but that's not how it seemed in the US, where the shock outweighed all excuses. British propaganda made much of the tragedy, comparing it to the murdered Belgian women and children, citizens of another neutral power. Nothing was said about the arms below deck.

The propaganda included a report by the former British ambassador to the US, Lord Bryce. Published less than a month after the Lusitania sinking, this outlined German "atrocities", particularly the execution of the British nurse Edith Cavell who had sheltered Belgian opponents of the Germans. The Kaiser had wished to pardon Miss Cavell but, influenced by his Anglophobic wife, was persuaded to sign her death warrant. Bryce's report contained exaggerations but he had been a popular ambassador and his report caused a stir in Washington.

In hindsight it is hard to believe the crassness with which Berlin handled Washington during the war. The Germans might have made much more of British brutality in incidents such as the execution of the leaders of the Easter Rising in Dublin in 1916, or of British arrogance in creating a black list of US companies trading with Germany. Germany's military competence often seemed in striking contrast with its clumsy diplomacy.

Colonel House, Woodrow Wilson's trusted adviser, was about to sit down to a dinner in London when he heard of the sinking of

CONSCIENTIOUS OBJECTORS

Before the First World War there had never been compulsory military service in Britain. The introduction of conscription in 1916 via the Military Service Act made pacifism a political issue for the first time.

The number of conscientious objectors was small – around 16,500.

They had to argue their case for exemption from conscription at local tribunals. The main reasons for refusing to fight some form of alternative service in place of military service, some working in dangerous conditions as stretcher-bearers and others at farming or in industry.* But a small minority of "absolutists" – such as the pacifist and religious writer Stephen Hobhouse – refused to do anything that might help the war effort, and were prepared to go to jail for their beliefs, where they were often treated brutally.

German U-boat UB 14 with its crew in the Black Sea in 1918

the Lusitania. He immediately telegrammed the president to say that "America has come to a parting of the ways, when she must determine whether she stands for civilized or uncivilized warfare. We can no longer remain neutral spectators." In September 1915, the Germans backed down; the U-Boats would henceforth abide by "cruiser rules". For now America stayed on the sidelines. But 18 months later Berlin changed its policy again – and this time Colonel House had his way.

CHAPTER TEN

THE TERRIBLE BATTLES OF 1916

By the beginning of 1917 the stalemate on the western front had lasted more than two years. Austria-Hungary and Russia were exhausted by the war. There were widespread shortages of food and fuel, with strikes and bread riots across the whole of Central and Eastern Europe. In March, riots in Petrograd in Russia brought down the Tsar's regime.

The western allies, however, were by no means ready to end the war; nor was Berlin, though the dreadful losses at Verdun and the Somme had taken their toll. In the first of these two terrible battles the Germans, determined to destroy the French army, attacked a fortress at Verdun in north eastern France. The fortress was strategically unimportant but the Germans calculated, rightly, that General

Joffre would be determined to hold it, and to regain it if he lost it. In the end he held it, but at a dreadful cost. When the battle ended, ten months after it had started, in December 1916, "the artillery of both sides had created a nightmare landscape such as the world had never before seen. To the horror was added that created by gas and flame-throwers in hand-to-hand war. Between them both sides lost half a million men." For many in France, the trauma of Verdun could not be forgotten, and the sense of malaise and demoralisation lingered after the war, contributing to the defeatism shown in 1940.

The Somme, Britain's first mass offensive of the war, was even bloodier. It began in July after a massive bombardment which lasted for a week. General Haig believed his preparations for the attack had been meticulous but the bombardment – with a million and a half shells fired – was a failure: a huge number of the shells were duds and those that reached their target failed to destroy the deep German defences.

By the end of the first day the British had 57,470 casualties of whom 21,392 died; almost half of the 120,000 men who went 'over the top' that terrible morning were killed or wounded. John Buchan, the novelist, was an observer when British troops, many of them scarcely trained, advanced across open fields. He wrote of a slow movement forward whose regularity was "astounding "; "the dead lay aligned as if on some parade".

More than four months later, by the end of the battle, and after the Allied armies had advanced a mere ten miles, British losses were 419,654, French losses 204,253. The battlefield had been churned, like that of Verdun, "into a featureless lunar landscape". As Michael Howard says, the Somme has become "in British group-memory, the epitome of incompetent generalship and pointless sacrifice".

Eighty per cent of Britain's 2.7 million war casualties occurred after July 1, 1916. The Somme, says John Keegan, "marked the end of an age of vital optimism in British life that has never been recovered".

Yet it was also a turning point in the war; the Germans suffered terribly, too. Their losses have been estimated at 680,000, though the figure has been fiercely disputed. A German staff officer wrote afterwards: "The Somme was the muddy grave of the German field army, and of the faith in the infallibility of German leadership." At home "the mighty German machine was beginning slowly but surely to run down". Even such a fierce nationalist as the writer Ernst Jünger, winner of the German equivalent of the Victoria Cross, admitted his side's weakening powers.

Many Germans were now desperate for peace; the potato crop had failed in autumn 1916 and food shortages were causing bread riots. The Social Democrats in the Reichstag had always been reluctant supporters of the war, but Germany's new military commanders, Paul von Hindenburg and Erich Ludendorff, had virtually taken control of the country, now more militaristic than ever. They were determined the war should go on, though waged more efficiently. A "Hindenburg Programme" made every man from 16 to 60 liable for war work.

How could the deadlock be broken? The German High Command, knowing there was no quick victory to be had on the Central Front, looked for the answer to the war at sea, or, more precisely, the war under it.

The threat from Germany's surface navy had always been contained. It was no match for the Royal Navy, which in August 1914 had 29 battleships to Germany's 18. Britain began enforcing a blockade, preventing vital supplies from reaching the Channel ports in Belgium, and did so relatively unhindered. Berlin knew that if its High Seas Fleet responded to the challenge to break the blockade by taking on Britain's Grand Fleet in a major battle, it could lose. The blockade was very effective; according to official German estimates after the war, 730,000 deaths were directly attributable to it.

At the end of May in 1916, a new German commander, Admiral Scheer, lost patience and led his fleet into battle with the Royal Navy. In what became known in Britain as the Battle of Jutland, he sank a total of 14 ships, while losing 11 of his own. In numerical terms, it may have been a victory, but it was a meaningless one, having no effect on the strategic picture. British ships continued to dominate the seas and the German fleet to rot in harbour. Right at the end of the war, when it was finally ordered out, the crews mutinied rather than be led by admirals into what would have been a "Death-Ride".

Admiral Scheer had always argued that the U-Boats were the best weapon with which to strike the British. During the first three years of the war Germany's submarine fleet grew rapidly, rising from 54 in 1915 to more than double that number. At the beginning of 1917, the German navy thought it was ready for a new campaign of unrestricted submarine warfare aimed at starving Britain into submission.

Two well-known German economists were "brought in to opine as to the damage that would be done to the British economy". They pronounced it would collapse – "especially if Zeppelins dropped bombs on the grain depots in the Channel ports, they helpfully added". Admiral Holtzendorff declared that he could sink 600,000 tons of shipping every month: that British shipping could be cut in half: that there would be food riots, and "terrible distress in the trading areas".

Germany's Chancellor, Bethmann-Hollweg, was sure that if Germany declared unrestricted submarine warfare the US would join the war. But against the military leadership, and with a population that "blamed its rat sausages and endless turnips on the British blockade", Bethmann-Hollweg could make no headway. "Smoking cigarette after cigarette he tried a manoeuvre to escape from the problem."

The manoeuvre, in December 1916, was to engage President Wilson in an attempt to find a formula for peace. But what should be the terms? The Entente did not want a peace dictated by America and the Germans did not want a public debate about their war aims. Bethmann-Hollwegg could not promise that Belgium would have her sovereignty restored because he had no intention of restoring it; the German navy was insistent that access to the Belgian Channel ports was vital for Germany's future security; and Generals Hindenburg and Ludendorff, dedicated to total victory, were now the real masters of Germany.

So Bethmann-Hollweg could offer little, "beyond silence and lies", and the initiative got nowhere. Germany's Chancellor had run out of options. His hand forced by the military, he rose in the Reichstag on February 1, 1917, to announce that a zone around western France and the British Isles would be open to sinking upon sight: "his voice was hoarse and rough. It was evidently very painful for him to plead for a policy which formerly he had passionately opposed."

CHAPTER ELEVEN

THE US JOINS THE WAR

Unrestricted submarine warfare was, as one German politician said, the Reich's last card, "and if it does not come up trumps, we are lost for centuries". At first it seemed that it might: with 105 submarines at his disposal, rising to 129 by the summer, Admiral Holtzendorff sank hundreds of thousands of tons of shipping in the next few months. "Neutrals began to withdraw, ships to be laid up, and American citizens were drowned." April was the worst month, with 881,000 tons going down, 545,000 of them British; during what was called the "black fortnight" hundreds of ships were sunk.

The early signs of success were deceptive. In 1915, one of the world's great physicists, the New Zealander Sir Ernest Rutherford (best known for splitting the atom), went out in a small boat on the Firth of Forth, accompanied by a colleague with perfect pitch. Taking a firm grip of his companion's ankles, Rutherford suspended him upside down with his head in the water, so that he could listen while a British submarine passed below. The companion, hauled back into the dinghy, said as he was towelling his head that he could identify the sound anywhere. Eventually, based on Rutherford's research, a hydrophone was invented, able to detect underwater noise.

Used with depth charges, hydrophones enabled destroyers to track and destroy submarines and this – along with the Admiralty's increasing use of convoys to protect merchant ships – led to a dramatic decline in the sinkings. The threat was contained but the U-Boats "had conjured up Germany's worst nightmare". They had more or less ensured that the United States would join the war.

It is just possible that despite the U-Boat campaign the arrival of American troops might have been averted. But there followed an episode which, in Norman Stone's view, ranks with the Schlieffen Plan and the decision to start a naval race with Britain "in the annals of German self-destructiveness". Berlin, feeling it must do something to try to counter US intervention, looked to Central America for a solution.

In 1916 John J. Pershing had led an American military expedition to Mexico to capture Pancho Villa, a bandit backed by the Germans. Mexico's resentment at the intervention led Arthur Zimmerman, the German foreign minister, to think that the Mexicans might "relish the opportunity to invade Texas". Zimmerman sent a message to Germany's ambassador in Washington, suggesting that he broach the idea of an alliance with Mexico in the event of American entry into the war. Unfortunately for Berlin, the threat backfired.

As early as August 5, 1914, a British cable ship had cut the transatlantic cable connecting Germany with the United States, meaning that the Germans could only communicate with their diplomats via cables that touched British territory or by wireless. Within four months of the war starting, Britain was in possession of Germany's naval codes. From then on, German radio traffic was monitored by naval intelligence, operating from Room 40 of the Old Admiralty Building in London, under its formidable director, Reginald "Blinker" Hall, so called, says Hew Strachan, "from his constant blinking, a habit his daughter somewhat improbably attributed to the terrible food at his preparatory school".

Zimmerman's message to the United States was sent by three different routes, and Room 40 intercepted all three. By February 17th, "Blinker" Hall was able to brief the US Ambassador in London. President Wilson then published the Zimmerman telegram as if Washington itself had managed to decipher it, thus protecting Room 40's secret role. The revelation convinced many doubting Americans that enough was enough.

The Tsar's abdication in March removed a further obstacle to America joining the war. The US had been reluctant to ally itself with an autocratic Russia and now it no longer needed to. On April 2nd, 1917, President Wilson said that the world "must be made safe for democracy"; the House of Representatives and the Senate voted for war by large majorities. Henceforth the vast reserves of US manpower and wealth made defeat almost certain for the Central Powers.

Crucially, America's decision ended the Alliance's dire financial problems. Britain had been subsidising Russia, and its credit was nearly exhausted; now the US government guaranteed the debt. Raw materials began to flow to the Allies and so, eventually, did soldiers, 200,000 a month by 1918. If the Allies could hold on, they would win.

The Germans were still hard to beat. After Russia's withdrawal from the war, and the Russian Revolution in November 1917, the revolutionary leader, Vladimir Ilyich Ulianov Lenin, had asked for an armistice and in December agreed to peace terms that were hugely favourable to Germany. Thanks to the Russian collapse 191 German divisions (where previously there had been 147) faced 179 Allied ones in the west. The Germans finally had superiority on the western front. In the first six months of 1918 Ludendorff made a last desperate bid for victory, launching major offensives against both the British and the French.

With food riots and strikes in Kiel and Berlin, and fears that the Russian example could prove infectious, Ludendorff knew he had little time. But his offensives, while briefly successful, could not prevail with 200,000 American soldiers joining the front every month. An Allied counter-offensive in July marked the beginning of the end.

While the military had become more powerful in Germany, strategic decisions in Paris and London were at this point being made by civilian governments rather than generals, and co-operation on the front between the Allies was better than it had been. Historians for the most part agree that both Marshal Foch (as he now was) and General Haig had learnt the lessons of earlier battles. The British army, says Michael Howard, "had made a remarkable recovery, and of no one was this more true than Haig himself. Haig's offensive

Heads of the "Big Four" nations at the Paris Peace Conference, 27 May 1919.
David Lloyd George, Vittorio Orlando, Georges Clemenceau and Woodrow Wilson

spirit, like that of Foch, had more often than not had disastrous consequences, but now, like that of Foch, its time had come."

Foch knew at last how the war could be won: suspend an attack when it succeeded; don't press on too far. The British army had learnt how to use tanks and to combine artillery and infantry more effectively. Low-flying aircraft posed much more of a threat than in the early days of the war. And, with the arrival of American forces, Allied forces were growing stronger by the week.

"There is a mysterious process in the defeat of any army – the point at which the men give up hope," says Norman Stone. In mid July the German army's morale began to break. During the Allied counter-offensive at Villers-Cotterets, the Kaiser asked Ludendorff what had gone wrong. The men were just not fighting any more, came the reply. Thousands were surrendering. Ludendorff's own nerve started to crack, too. "He began to hit the bottle and provoked quarrels with his subordinates." On September 29 he told the Kaiser that there was no hope of winning the war.

PART THREE:

<u>THE AFTERMATH</u>

The Hall of Mirrors in the Palace of Versailles, where Germany and the Allied Powers signed the Treaty of Versailles in 1919

CHAPTER TWELVE

WAS THE TREATY OF VERSAILLES FAIR?

Less than a week after hearing that there was no hope of a German victory, the Kaiser appointed as Chancellor the conciliatory figure of Prince Max of Baden, described by a senior American diplomat as "one of the few high Germans who seems to be able to think like a human being ". The appointment led, as unrest in Germany grew worse, to the dismissal of Ludendorff and then to the abdication of the Kaiser himself.

Prince Max asked President Wilson to take steps towards peace on the basis of the plan that the President had outlined the previous January. Had the Germans, instead of striving for victory, quickly sought to accept and adapt this plan – the President's famous "Fourteen Points", advocating self-determination and democracy – they might have achieved a different kind of peace. Instead, in the interim, they had imposed harsh terms on Russia, including the seizure of huge swathes of territory in eastern Europe. They had also killed some 114,000 American soldiers and sunk a passenger ship, the Leinster, as late as October 1918, with the loss of hundreds of British and American lives, causing the usually cool British Foreign Secretary, Arthur Balfour, to say: "Brutes they were and brutes they remain." In their retreat through Flanders, they had poisoned wells and "ringed" (thus killing) fruit-trees.

Woodrow Wilson was now the leader of a victorious alliance. He declared that the only armistice he would consider was one that would "leave the United States and the powers associated with her in a position to enforce any arrangements that might be entered into and make a renewal of hostilities on the part of Germany impossible".

In January 1919, when the world's statesmen converged on Paris, Europe was in ruins. The "Big Three", France, Britain and the USA, had different ambitions. France's Georges Clemenceau was determined to make France permanently secure by curbing Germany; Lloyd George didn't want to see France become too powerful; Woodrow Wilson wanted to remould the world on the basis of self-determination of peoples, as enshrined in his 14 points. Clemenceau is said to have remarked "that he was sitting between a would-be Napoleon (Lloyd George) and a would-be Jesus Christ (Wilson)". Lloyd George echoed this, with an important variation, when he arrived back in

England after the conference and was asked how he'd done: "Not badly, considering I was sitting between Jesus Christ and Napoleon."

But there were limits to the President's utopianism. "In his mind… the Germans had waged [a] war which defied the customs and conventions that defined relations between states." Wilson, like Lloyd George, was a liberal from a religious background: they both believed firmly "in chastising the wicked".

The terms of the treaty were tough. Alsace and Lorraine, seized by Germany in 1871, were to become French again, but Clemenceau's demand that the Rhineland be detached from Germany was blocked by Lloyd George; instead it was to be demilitarised. Germany was forbidden to unite with Austria; her handful of colonies were given to Britain and France as "mandates"; lands in east Germany were given to Poland. Germany was denied an air force and her army was to be limited to 100,000 men and forbidden to have tanks. The navy, too, was restricted. It was allowed six battleships and no submarines.

While most of the Treaty of Versailles's 440 clauses have been forgotten, the ones which are remembered are those which deal with reparations– the sum which Germany would have to pay for the damage that she had caused – and the clause which asserted German war guilt, justifying the reparations. These clauses, in the standard view, still stand as evidence of "a vindictive, short-sighted and poisonous document".

The new Weimar democracy started life with a crushing burden and the Nazis were able to play on understandable German resentment. Responsibility for the disastrous consequences, so the argument goes, starts with the peace-makers of 1919: the vengeful, grasping Clemenceau, the pusillanimous, vacillating Lloyd George and the pathetic, broken Wilson, who allowed himself, in the words of John Maynard Keynes to be bamboozled.

In the event, the final amount of the reparations was not decided at Versailles but by a special commission in London in 1921. Theoretically, this obliged the Germans to pay, in all, 132 billion gold marks (about £6.6bn, or $33bn) although the commission's report made clear they would in reality have to pay less than half that, with the rest due only if circumstances permitted.

What they actually ended up paying was a mere 22 billion gold marks (£1.1bn, $4.5bn), "probably slightly less than what France, with a much smaller economy, paid Germany after the Franco-Prussian War of 1870-71".

The idea that Versailles was a vindictive treaty was most vividly and persuasively argued by the economist John Maynard Keynes, a member of the British delegation. He resigned in protest at the harshness with which he believed Germany was being treated, then published what became a best-selling book, *The Economic Consequences of the Peace*, denouncing the treaty.

Keynes thought the peace terms "outrageous and impossible", threatening not just disorder and unrest but the possible destruction of capitalism in central Europe. "The policy of reducing Germany to servitude for a generation, of degrading the lives of millions of human beings, and of depriving a whole nation of happiness… [will] sow the decay of the whole civilised life of Europe."

The treaty, he declared, would complete Europe's economic

destruction. Wilson had betrayed the hopes of those who wanted a better world; Clemenceau was a dried-up, bitter old man, caring only for France and its security; Lloyd George was "this extraordinary figure of our time, this siren, this goat-footed bard, this half-human visitor to our age from the hag-ridden magic and enchanted woods of Celtic antiquity" (a ridiculous picture of the prime minister and of the Wales in which he grew up: although he liked to talk of his humble origins, Lloyd George came from the educated artisan class and was the son of a schoolmaster).

Was Keynes's view justified? Most modern historians think not. A better case is now made for the opposite contention: that the peace terms were not harsh enough. Margaret Macmillan wonders if Keynes's bitter verdict stemmed partly from guilt. Was he trying to atone for his support for the war with his pacifist Bloomsbury friends, some of whom laughed at his worldly success? His former lover, Lytton Strachey (a conscientious objector), had consist-

THE LEADERS OF 'THE BIG THREE'

What were they like, the three figures who came to Paris in 1919 to negotiate the peace treaty after the war: Woodrow Wilson, Clemenceau and Lloyd George?

The most puzzling was Wilson, says Margaret Macmillan in her much admired study of Versailles. A handsome man with fine features, the President of the United States was not really like the "cadaverous undertaker" that he appears to be in photographs. The son and grandson of Presbyterian ministers, he was greatly influenced by his upbringing and loved to quote the Bible.

But Wilson could be ruthless when crossed. Was he first and foremost an idealist? Or was he, as Teddy Roosevelt thought, "as insincere and cold-blooded an opportunist as we have ever had in the presidency"? (Macmillan, *The Peacemakers* p14) Clemenceau was the oldest of the three and though robust for his age suffered from eczema on his hands and chronic insomnia. He often woke at 3am and read until seven, when he made himself "a simple breakfast of gruel". (Macmillan, p40) He could be kind and generous but was determined not just to

ently taunted Keynes about his continuing involvement in the war effort. Macmillan quotes an American delegate: "Keynes got sore because they [the leaders at Versailles] wouldn't take his advice, his nerve broke, and he quit."

It is true that at the Peace Conference France's allies found Clemenceau exasperating, and his demand that Germany be crushed and dismembered unrealistic. But France had suffered the most; no other country lost a greater proportion of its population in the war. A quarter of French men between 18 and 30 died: more than 1.3 million out of a population of 40 million. In the north, "great stretches of land were pitted with shell holes, criss-crossed by trenches, marked with row upon row of crosses. Around the fortress of Verdun, site of the worst French battle, not a living thing grew, not a bird sang." As Clemenceau put it to Wilson: "America is far away, protected by the ocean. Not even Napoleon himself could touch England. You are both sheltered;

punish Germany but to keep the wartime alliance alive. Unfortunately, says Macmillan, he never established a good relationship with either Lloyd George or Woodrow Wilson. They would have small lunches together or drop in on each other; Clemenceau preferred to eat alone. His speeches had inspired the French particularly during the last year of the war. In March 1918 he had declared "My home policy: I wage war; my foreign policy: I wage war. All the time I wage war." He arrested "defeatists", putting them on trial for treason; those found guilty were executed in the moat at the Paris fort of Vincennes.

Lloyd George was the youngest of the three, "a cheerful, rosy-faced man with startling blue eyes and a shock of white hair. ('Hullo,' a little girl once asked him. 'Are you Charlie Chaplin?')" Clemenceau thought him ignorant; Lloyd George, for his part, thought the French Prime Minister a "disagreeable and rather bad-tempered old savage". Over time they warmed more to each other, though Lloyd George was not, insisted the old gentleman, "an English gentleman".

we are not."

It is true, too, that Wilson opposed heavy reparations but eventually backed down. Many believe that Lloyd George bamboozled him during the bitter arguments about how much Germany should pay, and to whom. Nor is it wrong to say that Lloyd George was slippery; he argued for high reparations with Wilson and Clemenceau but then, in his Fontainebleu Memorandum in March 1919, proposed moderation, arguing for a more lenient treaty which would not bring bitterness for years to come, encourage Germany to "throw in her lot with Bolshevism", and cause another war.

The more one examines it, the more the picture of a Germany crushed by a vindictive treaty falls apart. The Germans lost territory but had they won the war they would have imposed a much tougher peace on the losers, having already, as an American diplomat put it, "robbed Belgium… of every penny they [could] lay their hands on" and having set out to rob every country they attacked.

The argument that it would have been better simply to have blamed the Kaiser and his regime for the war, and to have welcomed the new Weimar Republic into the international fold, might sound plausible now. But in the febrile atmosphere after such terrible destruction, it was unthinkable. Anyway, public opinion (reflected in headlines and posters such as "Make the Hun pay") would not have worn it.

The trouble was that Versailles "brought about the worst of all worlds, an embittered Germany that was left strong enough to take revenge. A harsher peace, on the lines of 1945, would have been wiser…" There were all sorts of failures at Versailles – the League of Nations, set up by Wilson to adjudicate international problems, failed even to win support in the US Congress and soon declined "into irrelevance". But the greatest failure was not to have dealt conclusively with the German question. Germany was still too strong; there were 75 million Germans and only 40 million French, as Marshal Foch pointed out.

And most Germans didn't experience defeat at first hand. It has been argued that the worst mistake the allies made was not to occupy Germany; the reparations which the allies sought, thinks Norman Stone, could only really have been extracted from an occupied country, "as the Nazis displayed in France during the Second World War and as the European Economic Community did in Germany thereafter".

But in late 1918 there was no appetite for continuing the war. An exhausted Britain and France had been severely weakened and America, much less powerful than it was at the start of World War Two, had only stepped in with great reluctance.

The real problem with Versailles, perhaps, was the failure of the Allies to enforce it: war-weary, they lacked the necessary resolve. Arguably, Germany actually emerged in a better position following the treaty than before the war. Her eastern frontiers now faced Russia, weakened by revolution and civil war, and tiny Austria, which had lost its empire. France and Belgium to the west were smaller and economically weaker. The treaty therefore could be seen as enhancing German power.

By failing to partition Germany into smaller states, argues Correlli Barnett, Britain "had failed in her main purpose for taking part in the Great War". France's Marshal Foch told the New York Times that "next time" the Germans would not make a mistake. Predicting exactly what Hitler did 20 years later, he said they would "break through into northern France and seize the Channel ports as a base of operations against England".

The case against the Versailles treaty can be overstated. It has had a bad press but for all its imperfections, as Michael Howard has pointed out, most of its provisions "have stood the test of time". The new states it created (including Poland) have survived "if within fluctuating frontiers". It wasn't until the late 20th century that the Czechs and Slovaks peacefully separated and Yugoslavia split apart.

But the "German question" remained unresolved and, in spite of its defeat, Germany remained the most powerful country in Europe, with both France and Britain haunted by the prospect of another dreadful war, and the United States, its intervention in Europe widely thought to have been a mistake, determined not to repeat it. The peacemakers made mistakes, says Margaret Macmillan, and their "offhand treatment of the non-European world… stirred up resentments for which the West is still paying today". This is particularly true of the Middle East, where they threw together peoples, most notably in Iraq, who were unlikely ever to cohere into workable societies. But they took pains over the borders in Europe and tried, "even cynical old Clemenceau", to build a better order.

Some believe that in the 20th century there was only one war, which lasted from 1914 to 1945 with a long armistice in the middle and which, in the end, gave Russia and America a dominant role in Europe. There is some truth in this, though to argue that the Treaty of Versailles "caused" World War Two is too simplistic; without the Wall Street Crash of 1929, and the consequent Great Depression, it is conceivable that war in 1939 might have been averted. It was the economic crisis and unemployment which enabled Hitler to rise to power.

Many Germans subscribed, as he did, to the theory that the country had been 'stabbed in the back': "Jews, the Left, soft-brained academics had prevented them from winning the war…" The worse Germany's economic plight became, the more it was blamed on reparations, and on Versailles. German Foreign Office officials wrote study after study criticising the treaty; their views were echoed in the Munich beer halls where the young Hitler denounced the "peace of shame". The fact that Germany had been forced to sign the treaty without even knowing the cost of reparations seemed to compound the unfairness.

In the last days of the war, when armistice terms were discussed, Lloyd George said: "if peace were made now, in twenty years' time the Germans would say what Carthage had said about the First Punic War, namely that they had made this mistake and that mistake, and by better preparation and organization they would be able to bring about victory next time". This was more or less what Hitler later did say – in *Mein Kampf.* It was already his view in November, 1918, as he lay, convalescing, after being gassed. "Did all this happen so a gang of wretched criminals could lay hands on the fatherland?"

CHAPTER THIRTEEN

HOW THE WAR CHANGED EUROPE

Four empires fell: the German empire, the Austro-Hungarian empire, the Russian empire and the Ottoman empire. New countries – some revived after centuries – rose out of the peace treaties: Czechoslovakia, Hungary, Poland, an enlarged Yugoslavia, Estonia, Latvia, Lithuania. Germany lost territory on her eastern frontiers to the new Poland and the new Czechoslovakia; Romania, Italy, Poland and Czechoslovakia gained land from the former Austria-Hungary, Austria (forbidden union with Germany) became the rump of a once huge empire. Britain and France divided the former Ottoman possessions: Syria and the Lebanon to France; Palestine and the new countries of Jordan and

Iraq to Britain.

Ethnic groups were stranded: Germans in northern Czechoslovakia and in Lithuania and Poland; Lithuanians in Poland; Hungarians in an enlarged Romania. It has been estimated that about 30 million people found themselves on the wrong side of frontiers. The post-Ottoman Middle East became even more explosive, with incompatible forms of Islam, Britain's promise to make a Jewish national home alongside the Arabs in Palestine, the West's determination to control the oil and resentment at further colonisation.

Indian troops had fought in the war. Had this service to the distant King Emperor been worthwhile if it brought no change to their position under British rule? Australians had died at Gallipoli. Was Britain's cause theirs? Why had they been fighting?

Then there was the experience. Millions of young men were taken out of what had been for the most part poor and restricted peacetime lives. They went abroad for the first time and suffered great danger, often commanded by officers who were scarcely out of adolescence. There was courage and endurance, in dire conditions, under remote generals who could seem oblivious of reality. A sense of comradeship grew; the poets who loathed the slaughter such as Siegfried Sassoon, Ivor Gurney and Edmund Blunden cherished the memory of wartime friendships. Blunden thought that he would never see such kindness again.

> When will the stern fine "Who goes there?"
> Meet me again in midnight air?
> And the gruff sentry's kindness, when
> Will kindness have such power again?

Deference was fatally wounded in the trenches, with the working classes coming into much closer contact with those who had once been thought to be their natural superiors. The view of women changed – how they were seen, how they saw themselves – to encompass much more than domestic service or wifely duties. Many more worked in factories, farms or offices, replacing men who had gone to fight. It no longer seemed credible to deny them the vote.

Britain saw much greater state control. Alfred Pollard, Professor of Constitutional History at the University of London, suggested in August 1917 that the country had succumbed to the Prussianism it was meant to be fighting. Pollard imagined how a "Prussian" might speak to England, saying: "We were right after all, and in practice you admit it by manifold imitation. You have adopted conscription, gagged your Press, suspended your constitutional guarantees and your sacred rights of liberty."

The new, shrill nationalism of the Press seemed "unBritish". In the House of Commons, the Conservative Colonel Aubrey Herbert, who had fought on the western front, criticised "the brutish Prussian attitude of our own Yellow Press..." The poet Siegfried Sassoon, also an officer, wrote of wanting to make "the Yellow-Pressmen grunt and squeal".

Germany, a country without historically proven institutions, had staked all on war. Anything short of outright victory was certain to threaten her political stability, if only because of the huge role of the army in German national life. The country was a blend of militarism, democracy (the franchise was wider than in Britain, with the German Socialist party the largest in Europe) and autocracy. The Kaiser was deeply involved in politics, having immense power in defence and foreign affairs and the choice of ministers.

But defeat meant political collapse: by 1917 both the Kaiser and the Reichstag had been sidelined and there was a military dictatorship run by Generals Hindenburg and Ludendorff. In 1918 Kaiser Wilhelm II, though some believed he should be put on trial for war crimes, was allowed to go into exile to a pleasant villa in Holland, where his first request was for a cup of good English tea. There he wrote his memoirs, brooded over his old medals and uniforms, read P.G. Wodehouse and watched Hitler's "succession of miracles" with delight until he died in 1941.

Defeat was also catastrophic for Russia, beaten by the Central Powers and exploding into revolution in 1917. The Hapsburg rule could not last in a defeated Austria-Hungary. In Turkey the last Sultan was replaced by a secular republic. By the end of the war, the Romanovs, Hapsburgs and Hohenzollerns had all gone.

The war, as Niall Ferguson says, was "a turning point in the long-running conflict between monarchism and republicanism". On the eve of it, descendants and other relations of Queen Victoria had sat on the thrones not only of Great Britain and Ireland, but also of Austria-Hungary, Russia, Germany, Belgium, Romania, Greece and Bulgaria. In Europe there were only three republics: France, Portugal and Switzerland: "the letters exchanged between 'George' [in Britain], 'Willy' [in Germany] and 'Nicky' [in Russia] testify to the continuing existence of a cosmopolitan, multi-lingual royal elite with at least some sense of collective interest". The post-war map saw the emergence of republics in Russia, Germany, Austria, Hungary, Czechoslovakia, Poland, the three Baltic states and, eventually, in Southern Ireland. "This must rank as one of the least intended consequences of the war," says Ferguson. "In

Russia, moreover, the new republic was a tyranny far more blood-thirsty and illiberal than that of the tsars."

It was a war in which the victors paid a terrible price. The losses were huge, in the millions of young dead, in the damaged infrastructure, in massive war debts. There was a horror of future wars, particularly in countries which lacked the impetus of revenge or felt the humiliation of defeat. Nearly ten million soldiers died, an average of around 6,046 every day; twice that number were wounded. Many civilians died, too, and in the immediate aftermath an influenza epidemic swept through Asia, Europe and America killing 20 million more. The bereaved were not forgotten. "Every day one meets saddened women, with haggard faces and lethargic movements, and one dare not ask after husband or son," wrote Beatrice Webb in her diary on November 17, 1918.

Nationalism, far from ending with the war, was inflamed by it, especially in Germany. There were many reasons for Germany's sense of affronted national pride and humiliation: the bill for reparations; the surge of inflation, caused by the printing of vast quantities of money; the still armed, demobbed soldiers drifting without work; the French occupation of the Ruhr; the myth that an unconquered Germany had had defeat imposed upon her by treacherous politicians.

A symbol of this was the huge Tannenberg Memorial, planned soon after the war and dedicated in 1927 by Hindenburg, then the President of Germany, who rejected the so-called "guilt" clause in the Treaty of Versailles which said that Germany had caused the war. The ceremony became an assertion of nationalism as medals shone on resuscitated uniforms and speeches became bombastic. The huge building was itself a shrine to conquest, resembling a fortress of the Teutonic knights.

The Russians were savages; the English, sly manipulators; the Germans, monsters; the French, unreliable and vengeful: such ideas of nations emerge in political speeches and polemics after 1918. In his ghosted post-war memoirs, Hindenburg showed England as a land of devious hypocrites, working nefariously to get her way, fearful of outright confrontation. So the caricature view of peoples and countries grew even sharper, even more hateful. The moral power of the League of Nations faded.

One of the many depressing aspects of the First World War is that it settled so little. For the independent countries that emerged after 1918, it had been, in a terrible way, necessary; Poland, Czechoslovakia and the new Baltic States would not have existed without the war. But even here the business was unfinished for it took most of the rest of the century to ensure their lasting freedom. Much of the Middle East simply passed from one empire to another. The small group of statesmen, diplomats and generals, the old elite, who failed to stop the slide towards the explosion of August 1914 were innocents compared to the monsters who came later. But they ensured the end of Europe as the centre of the world.

THE WAR POETS

Poetry was there from the start of the war, in all the combatant countries, even in the United States which stayed neutral until 1917. Germany is said to have produced more than a million war poems in 1914. In Britain, The Times was inundated with poetry, with established figures such as Robert Bridges, Thomas Hardy and Henry Newbolt appearing alongside younger writers.

Rupert Brooke, whose work had already been praised, joined up quickly, believing that his task now was "to kill Germans", especially since seeing the chaos of a British attempt in October 1914 to save Antwerp from the enemy. His war sonnets appeared early in 1915. One of these, "The Soldier" ("If I should die, think only this of me...."), has remained one of the best known poems of the 20th century, achieving fame when the Dean of St Paul's quoted from it in his 1915 Easter sermon. By then, Brooke, bound for Gallipoli, was dying from an infected mosquito bite. He was buried on the Greek island of Skyros, putting his brother officers in mind of the young Achilles. Brooke's last poem, found among his papers, shows that his excitement was fading into anxiety.

Wilfred Owen, who won the Military Cross for courage and leadership in 1918

In November 1915 Siegfried Sassoon arrived at the front as a young officer. Soon Sassoon's poetry, previously euphoric, even after his brother had been killed at Gallipoli, was describing angrily what the men endured.

> *If I were fierce and bold, and short of breath,*
> *I'd live with scarlet Majors at the Base,*
> *And speed glum heroes up the line to death.*
> *You'd see me with my puffy petulant face,*
> *Guzzling and gulping in the best hotel,*
> *Reading the Roll of Honour.*
> *"Poor young chap," I'd say – "I used to know his father well;*
> *Yes, we've lost heavily in this last scrap."*
> *And when the war is done and youth stone dead,*
> *I'd toddle off safely home and die – in bed.*

Sassoon was a brave officer, wanting, like Brooke, to kill Germans (particularly after the death of a close friend) and winning the Military Cross. Even after his protest against the war, for which he was sent to Craiglockhart hospital in Edinburgh, having been declared to be suffering from shell shock, he returned to the front and his solitary nocturnal patrols in No Man's Land.

During the last weeks of the war, the poet Wilfred Owen was killed during an attack on the Sambre Canal, having also won the Military Cross. His poems are often quoted as an example of war's futility but Owen declared that he hated pacifists almost as much as Prussian militarists. He told his mother during his last months how he had fought "like an angel", accounting for several of the enemy.

The expression of war's agony in Sassoon and Owen's work reflected individual experience rather than a wish for peace at any price. These poets loathed the armchair militants of the home front rather than the actual fighting. They despised non-combatants who could have no idea of what the soldiers endured. Owen told his mother in his last letter from the front that there was no place where he would rather be.

Neither Owen nor Sassoon reached a large readership during the war. It was those who showed patriotism or dutiful determination who sold best: poets such as Rupert Brooke and John Oxenham whose real name was William Dunkerly. Dunkerly was a successful grocer who took up poetry and his collection *All's Well*, published in November 1915, soon after the battle of Loos, sold 75,000 copies by July 1916, the first month of the battle of the Somme. His writing was strongly Christian and had a nostalgia for peace, but he didn't shirk war's horrors and celebrated the stoicism that, he believed, would take Britain through to victory.

During the 1920s, the war occupied only a small place in the literary landscape; it was as if people wanted either to forget or to move on. Then at the end of the decade came a fusillade of prose memoirs, including those by Sassoon, Robert Graves and Edmund Blunden. Auden, Spender and Day Lewis – left-wing poets of the 1930s, a time of economic crisis and dictators – admired Owen; his sales, however, stayed modest. Sassoon had more fame for his semi-fictional autobiographies such as the *Memoirs of a Fox-hunting Man* and *Memoirs of an Infantry Officer* that tell of innocence blown apart on the western front.

Some politicians and historians believed the war poets and writers had a disastrous influence on the moral fibre of Britain. Did the war books published at the end of the 1920s turn people against the idea of any confrontation with Germany? Did they prompt the question: is peace always better than war? Were the poets partly responsible for the appeasement of Hitler?

Siegfried Sasson lived through both wars, and was Owen's mentor in poetry

THE HOME FRONT

The First World War was the first "total war", says Roger Chickering: it affected every aspect of the life of the countries involved. During the Second World War, ten civilians were killed for every soldier; during the Great War, nine soldiers were killed for every civilian – yet these civilian deaths were still critical to public opinion.

Germany had superiority in the air and brought the war to Allied civilians with Zeppelin and bomber raids. From 1914 to 1918 Britain had 103 air raids, with 1,414 deaths and 3,416 injured. These deaths confirmed the British view that they were fighting monsters. The lawyer Edward Heron-Allan wrote in September 1915 that Londoners had "never dreamed such a thing would occur in England". What might come next? It was possible to imagine endless destruction.

A robust home front was vital for victory, and food supply was key. In 1914, Germany and Britain, unlike France (still overwhelmingly an agricultural country) were substantial importers of food. Years of free trade had made Britain an increasing consumer of cheap American and Canadian grain, to the neglect of her own agriculture. Yet Britain succeeded in protecting her imports due to the superiority of her navy. France and Britain also co-operated more effectively over trade and supply than the Central Powers. Britain produced enough coal to supply France, whose coalfields were occupied by the Germans.

Britain – to the surprise of German prisoners of war – became even better fed during the war than in peacetime. She was forced to introduce rationing for sugar, meat, bread, jam and tea in 1918 and bread "grew greyer", but this was nothing compared to the widespread hunger experienced in Austria-Hungary and Germany towards the end of the war.

The Central Powers had the advantage of geography. They were in one block, making movement between them easier, and benefited from the superb German railway network. But there were civilian deaths in Germany, particularly during the starvation of the so-called Turnip Winter of 1916-17, blamed on the Royal Navy's blockade. Propaganda showed England as the instigator of hunger and misery, citing the Irish famine of the 1840s when it was claimed England had turned Ireland into a place of "murder, hunger and forced deportation". Other propaganda included a short film that showed Russian Cossacks burning peaceful farms in East Prussia, paving the way for the punishing peace that was imposed on Russia by Germany early in 1918.

Industrial production – of armaments and machines – was nearly as vital to victory as a good food supply. The home front supremos – such as Sir Joseph Maclay in Britain or Walter Rathenau in Germany – were arguably as important as the generals. They were given unprecedented powers: in Britain, the Defence of the Realm Act, passed in 1914, allowed the government totake over coalmines, railways and shipping.

British industry responded well. In 1910 the Vickers ship building and arms works in Barrow employed 10,000 people; by 1918 the number had reached 30,000. At first the pre-war strikes faded, with the trades unions infected by the new national unity. There were, however, strikes in later years – of munitions workers in Glasgow in 1915, for example, and in Barrow in 1917.

Prices rose quickly in Britain during the war and goods became scarce, but pay increased and more jobs became available as men left for the front. Women became firemen, coalmen, bus conductors and "munitionettes", producing arms in the munitions factories. Robert Roberts remembers that in Salford by late 1916 "poverty began to disappear from the neighbourhood… children looked better fed" and women "appeared less unkempt and better dressed". The historian William Woodruff, who grew up in working-class Black-burn, wrote of the Lancashire textile mills that nothing helped the industry so much as the war. 1918 "was the most prosperous in the industry's history", with plenty to eat at last.

Germany, despite it reputation for efficiency, could not over-come the challenges posed by prolonged war, naval blockade and the economic strength of the Allies. Deprivation was intensified during the Hindenburg Programme of the last two years of the war, and even the plunder of occupied territories – Poland and Belgium – could not bring relief. Often, government intervention actually made things worse: the government tried to alleviate the grain shortage by slaughtering nine million pigs in 1915; in doing so they removed a vital source of food and fertiliser, deepening hunger.

A BRIEF CHRONOLOGY

1914

July 14 — Assassinations of the Archduke Franz Ferdinand and his wife Sophie at Sarajevo.

July 28 — Austria declares war on Serbia.

August 1 — Germany declares war on Russia and France.

August 4 — Britain declares war on Germany.

September 25 — Start of the battle of the Marne and the end of the German advance in the west.

1915

April 25 — British and French forces land at Gallipoli.

May 23 — Italy declares war on Germany and Austria.

December 19 — Allies begin to evacuate Gallipoli.

1916

February 21 — Germans begin their attacks at Verdun.

May 31 — Battle of Jutland.

July 1 — Battle of the Somme begins and lasts through the Autumn.

1917

February 1	Germany launches an unrestricted U boat campaign.
April 6	The United States declares war on Germany.
April 9	Start of the British and French offensive around Arras in France.
July 31	Start of the British offensive in Flanders that lasts through the Autumn.
November 8	Lenin and Bolsheviks take power in Russia.

1918

March 3	Treaty of Brest-Litovsk signed between Germany and Russia.
March 21	Start of last German offensive on the western front.
July 20	German retreat begins on the Marne.
November 3	Austria signs an armistice with the Allies
November 11	Germany signs an armistice with the Allies.

1919

January 12	Peace conference opens in Paris.
June 28	Signing of the treaty in the Hall of Mirrors at Versailles.

FURTHER READING

Blunden, Edmund. *Undertones of War (London 1928)*

Clark, Christopher. *The Sleepwalkers, How Europe Went to War in 1914* (London 2012)

Egremont, Max. *Some Desperate Glory, The First World War the Poets Knew* (London 2014)

Graves, Robert. *Goodbye to All That* (London 1929)

Hastings, Max. *Catastrophe, Europe Goes to War 1914* (London 2013)

Hibberd, Dominic and John Onions (ed). *The Winter of the World, Poems of the First World War* (London 2007)

Holmes, Richard. *Tommy, The British Soldier on the Western Front 1914-18* (London 2004)

Howard, Michael. *The First World War, A Very Short Introduction* (Oxford 2007)

Lieven, Dominic. *Towards the Flame, Empire, War and the End of Tsarist Russia* (London 2015)

Macmillan, Margaret. *Peacemakers* (London 2001)

Macmillan, Margaret. *The War that Ended Peace* (London 2013)

Owen, Wilfred. *Poems* (London 2004)

Röhl, John. *Wilhelm II: Into the Abyss of War and Exile 1900-1941* (Cambridge 2014)

Sassoon, Siegfried. *Memoirs of a Fox-hunting Man* (London 1928)

Sassoon, Siegfried. *Memoirs of an Infantry Officer* (London 1930)

Sassoon, Siegfried. *The War Poems* (London 1983)

Sheffield, Gary. *A Short History of World War One* (London 2014)

Stern, Fritz. *The Failure of Illiberalism* (London 1972)

Stone, Norman. *World War One, A Short History* (London 2008)

Walter, George (ed.). *The Penguin Book of First World War Poetry* (London 2006)

Watson, Alexander. *Ring of Steel, Germany and Austria-Hungary at War 1914-1918* (London 2014)

END NOTES

Chapter One:
Why was the rise of Germany so dangerous?

10 "as the loosest of cannons" Gary Sheffield, *A Short History of World War One*, p4

10 "archaic militarism" Michael Howard, *A Very Short Introduction to the First World War*, p9

11 "wild cards in the doom game" Max Hastings, *Catastrophe*, p6

11 He was an extreme exemplar… Christopher Clark, *The Sleepwalkers*, p182

11 "Bismarck…left a system which only he" Jonathon Steinberg, *Bismark: A Life*, p458

13 "That young man (the Kaiser)" John Rohl, Young Wilhelm: *The Kaiser's Early Life*, p813

14 "In 1914, Berlin was the Athens of the world" Norman Stone, *A Short World War One History*, p7

14 "In 1914 the great smokestacks of the Ruhr predominated" Stone, p8

Chapter Two:
What was the effect of the Kaiser's plan for a powerful navy?

15 'His "model" was rich Britain with her huge empire'

16 "the greatest mistake" Stone, p11

16 "Although there were other milestones" Sheffield, p6

18 "weaving a web to encircle and imprison them" Howard, p13

Chapter Three:
How culpable was Austria-Hungary?

21 "Deputies blew trumpets" Margaret Macmillan, *The war that ended peace*, p211

23 "In an age of nationalism," Stone, p21

24 "Please leave the small door unlocked." Hastings, p9

24 "Its officer corps was dominated by nobleman," Ibid

24 "regarded war with reckless insouciance," Hastings, p11

Chapter Four:
Was Serbia a rogue state?

27 "were irritated by its little Serbia proud-victim culture". Hastings, p17

27 "firing at cabinets," Clark, p3

27 "cut down in a hail of shots" Clark, p4

28 The king was really the "prisoner"… Clark, p14

28 "reminded admirers of broad-shouldered" Clarke, p11

29 "the most formidable document" Sheffield, p13

29 "seems extravagant," Hastings, p45

29 "where he produced melancholy pencil sketches" Macmillan, p218

30 "one of the most intriguing figures" Clark, p101

32 " to overstate the importance of this relationship" Clark, p104

32 "it nevertheless twirled smartly into sharp points" Macmillan, p213

32 "shot all 200 of them" Macmillan, p213

33 "not permitted to join her husband" Clark, p107

33 "that in assassinating Franz Ferdinand" Macmillan, p21533X "represented the best justification" Hastings, p42

33 "It is clear that a large measure" Sheffield, p14

Chapter Five: How much was Germany to blame?

39 This view - that Germany's domestic troubles... Sheffield, p18

41 "Germany was the aggressor..." Niall Ferguson, The Pity of War, pxli

Chapter Six: Was Britain right to join in?

42 "banging on the table:" Stone, p19

43 "Railways won wars." Stone, p26

43 "like drawing a gun;" Howard, p24

43 "to acquiesce in a German hegemony of Europe" Howard, p21

43 Not to do so... Howard, p24

44 "who must be faced down" Howard, p21

45 "you have your information" Hastings, p67

46 "Germany, the model country," Stone, p28

46 "Had Germany not invaded Belgium" Howard, p22

47 "deplorable record of inhumanity" Hastings, p90

47 It's also unfair to Grey who... Sheffield, p24

50 "a systematic attempt to impose its will," Hastings, Radio Times, 24th February 2014

50 "The outbreak of war" Clark, p561

51 Ferguson's "Panglossian view" Sheffield, p24

Chapter Seven: Why did the Schlieffen Plan fail?

56 "although the new weapons" Howard, p17

57 "No war has ever begun" Stone, p26

57 "the most important government document" John Keegan, The First World War, p31

57 The Chief of the General Staff was always on duty... For a German post-war view of Schlieffen and his plan, see Hermann von Kuhl,

Der Deutsche Generalstab in Vorbereitung und Durchführung des Weltkrieges (Berlin 1920)

58 "surrounding and annihilating" Howard, p30

58 "having been stuffed into fortresses". Stone, p41

59 They endured heavy losses to the north,... Howard, p31

60 "the vast fallacy of Schlieffen" Hastings, p314

60 "millions of men," Hastings, p314

60 "geared to the wrong century" Roger Chickering, *Imperial Germany and the Great War*, 1912-1918, p29

61 Joffre, on the other hand,... Sheffield, p37

62 "the army itself had been undefeated" Hew Strachan, *The First World War*, p59

Chapter Eight: Were Britain's soldiers led by donkeys?

65 "a captious and jealous rigidity" Ferguson, p303

65 "has received such mockery" Max Hastings, introduction to C.S. Forester's *The General*

67 "we went into this war lacking preparation" Ferguson, p305

69 "offered a penetrating study of" Hastings, Introduction, The General

69 "The Western Front's dominant reality" Hastings, Introduction, The General

71 The Russians endured horrendous losses... Howard, p52

72 "doubtful how much longer" Ferguson, p304

72 Between 1914 and 1918,... Strachan, p171, Keegan, p338

73 "were spared the odium" Hastings, Introduction, *The General*

Chapter Ten:
What were the effects of the terrible battles of 1916?

79 Austria-Hungary and Russia were exhausted by the war. Howard, p68

80 "the artillery of both sides" Howard, p64

80 "in British group-memory," Howard, p65

81 "the mighty German machine" John William, The Home Fronts, 1914-1918, p227

81 A "Hindenburg Programme" Stone, p118

82 Berlin knew that if its… Stone, p196

82 "brought in to opine" Stone, p120

83 "terrible distress in" Stone, p121

83 "Smoking cigarette after" Stone, p121

83 The Entente did not want… Strachan, p219

83 "It was evidently very painful" Strachan, p220

Chapter Eleven: Why did the US finally decide to fight?

84 "and if it does…" Howard, p72

84 "Neutrals began to withdraw" Stone, p123

85 "had conjured up Germany's" Stone, p124

85 Zimmerman sent a message… Strachan, p220

86 "from his constant blinking" Strachan, p199

87-88 "Haig's offensive spirit" Howard, p106

88 In mid July the German… Stone, p172

88 "He began to hit the bottle" Stone, p173

Chapter Twelve:
How fair was the Treaty of Versailles?

91 Woodrow Wilson wanted to remould the world… Sheffield, p173

92 "In his mind" Strachan, p323

92 "in chastising the wicked". Margaret Macmillan, The Peacemakers, p171

92 "The new Weimar democracy" Macmillan, The Peacemakers, p192

93 "probably slightly less" Macmillan, The Peacemakers, p192

Chapter Fourteen:
How did the First World War change Europe?

INDEX